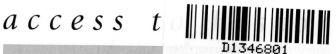

access t ...... history

From **BISMARCK** *to* **HITLER**

Second Edition

Geoff Layton

Hodder & Stoughton

A MEMBER OF THE HODDER HEADLINE GROUP

Acknowledgements

The cover illustration is Hindenburg by Hugo Vogel from Bildarchiv Preussischer Kulturbesitz.

The Publishers would like to thank the following for permissions to reproduce material in this volume:

A J Nicholls, Weimar and the Rise of Hitler, 1968, Palgrave Macmillan, reproduced with permission of Palgrave Macmillan; Modern European History by K Perry, reprinted by permission of Elsevier Science Ltd.; Telegraph Group Limited for extracts from the interview with Colonel Stuart Wortley; Cambridge University Press for extracts from John C G Röhl & Nicolaus Sombart, Kaiser Wilhelm II New Interpretations The Corfu Papers, 1982, Cambridge University Press.

The Publishers would like to thank the following for permission to reproduce copyright illustrations in this volume:

AKG Photo, page 40; The Imperial War Museum, page 67; AKG London, pages 96, 147; The Wiener Library, page 117; David Low and The Star and for supply of photo on page 150; Centre for the Study of Cartoons and Caricature, University of Kent, Canterbury, CT2 7NU, Kent.

Every effort has been made to trace and acknowledge ownership of copyright. The Publishers will be glad to make suitable arrangements with any copyright holders whom it has not been possible to contact.

Orders: please contact Bookpoint Ltd, 130 Milton Park, Abingdon, Oxon OX14 4SB. Telephone (44) 01235 827720, Fax: (44) 01235 400454. Lines are open from 9.00–6.00, Monday to Saturday, with a 24 hour message answering service. Email address: orders@bookpoint.co.uk

British Library Cataloguing in Publication Data
A catalogue record for this title is available from the British Library

ISBN 0 340 802057

First published 2002
Impression number   10 9 8 7 6 5 4 3 2 1
Year   2007 2006 2005 2004 2003 2002

Copyright © 2002

Typeset by Fakenham Photosetting Limited, Fakenham, Norfolk
Printed in Great Britain for Hodder & Stoughton Educational, a division of Hodder Headline Plc, 338 Euston Road, London NW1 3BH by Bath Press Ltd.

Contents

Preface   v

Chapter 1   Introduction   1
                1 Unification and Bismarck's Germany   1
                2 The Legacy of Bismarck   2
                3 Bismarck's Constitution   4
                Study Guide   7

Chapter 2   The Structure of Imperial Germany, 1890–1914   9
                1 Economic and Social Change   9
                2 The German Banking System and the
                  Development of Cartels   12
                3 German Society   13
                4 The Political System   15
                5 The *Reichstag*   23
                6 Political Forces within Wilhelmine Germany   27
                Study Guide   30

Chapter 3   The Domestic Policies of Imperial Germany,
                1890–1914   33
                1 Domestic Affairs, 1890–1914   33
                2 *Weltpolitik* and Domestic Policy   35
                3 The *Daily Telegraph* Affair   38
                4 Political Developments During the Years
                  Before the Outbreak of War   41
                5 The Crises of 1912–13   42
                Study Guide   45

Chapter 4   German Foreign Policy, 1890–1914. The
                  Origins of the First World War   48
                1 Germany and the European Situation   48
                2 The Coming of *Weltpolitik*, 1897–1907   51
                3 The Road to War   53
                4 1911–1914: The Last Years of Peace   54
                5 July 1914: Germany Goes to War   55
                6 Conclusion: The War – Who was Responsible?   58
                Study Guide   60

Chapter 5   Germany and the First World War, 1914–18   64
                1 The Opening Moves   64
                2 The Course of the War   67
                3 The Home Front   68
                4 The Latter Stages of the War, 1917–18   72
                5 The Domestic Impact of War   74
                6 The Home Front – the Human Experience   79
                7 Germany's War Aims   81
                Study Guide   86

Chapter 6   The German Revolution, 1918–19   88
                1 October–November 1918 – The Political Situation 88
                2 The Birth of the German Republic   90
                3 Conclusion   95
                Study Guide   97

Chapter 7   Weimar: The Years of Crisis, 1919–24   100
                1 The Political Situation in Post-War Germany   100
                2 The Weimar Constitution   102
                3 The Treaty of Versailles   105
                4 The Economic and Social Crisis, 1919–23   110
                5 The Political Crisis   117
                6 Stresemann and the 'Miracle of the
                  Rentenmark'   123
                Study Guide   126

Chapter 8   Weimar: Years of Relative Stability, 1924–29   129
                1 The Economic Situation   130
                2 Political Recovery   134
                3 Weimar Foreign Policy   138
                4 The Stresemann Years   140
                5 The Weimar Republic 1924–9 – An Overview   146
                Study Guide   149

Chapter 9   Weimar: The Final Years, 1929–33   153
                1 The World Economic Crisis   154
                2 Heinrich Bruning, Chancellor 1930–2   156
                3 The Rise of National Socialism   163
                4 The Final Months of the Weimar Republic   165
                5 Why Did Weimar Democracy Fail?   166
                Study Guide   169

Glossary   165
Further Reading   166
Index   168

Preface

To the general reader

Although the *Access to History* series has been designed with the needs of students studying the subject at higher examination levels very much in mind, it also has a great deal to offer the general reader. The main body of the text (i.e. ignoring the 'Study Guides' at the ends of Chapters) forms a readable and yet stimulating survey of a coherent topic as studied by historians. However, each author's aim has not merely been to provide a clear explanation of what happened in the past (to interest and inform): it has also been assumed that most readers wish to be stimulated into thinking further about the topic and to form opinions of their own about the significance of the events that are described and discussed (to be challenged). Thus, although no prior knowledge of the topic is expected on the reader's part, she or he is treated as an intelligent and thinking person throughout. The author tends to share ideas and possibilities with the reader, rather than passing on numbers of so-called 'historical truths'.

To the student reader

Although advantage has been taken of the publication of a second edition to ensure the results of recent research are reflected in the text, the main alteration from the first edition is the inclusion of new features, and the modification of existing ones, aimed at assisting you in your study of the topic at AS level, A level and Higher. Two features are designed to assist you during your first reading of a chapter. The *Points to Consider* section following each chapter title is intended to focus your attention on the main theme(s) of the chapter, and the issues box following most section headings alerts you to the question or questions to be dealt with in the section. The *Working on. . .* section at the end of each chapter suggests ways of gaining maximum benefit from the chapter.

There are many ways in which the series can be used by students studying History at a higher level. It will, therefore, be worthwhile thinking about your own study strategy before you start your work on this book. Obviously, your strategy will vary depending on the aim you have in mind, and the time for study that is available to you.

If, for example, you want to acquire a general overview of the topic in the shortest possible time, the following approach will probably be the most effective:

1. Read Chapter 1. As you do so, keep in mind the issues raised in the *Points to Consider* section.
2. Read the *Points to Consider* section at the beginning of Chapter 2 and decide whether it is necessary for you to read this chapter.
3. If it is, read the chapter, stopping at each heading or sub-heading to note

down the main points that have been made. Often, the best way of doing this is to answer the question(s) posed in the Key Issues boxes.
4. Repeat stage 2 (and stage 3 where appropriate) for all the other chapters.

If, however, your aim is to gain a thorough grasp of the topic, taking however much time is necessary to do so, you may benefit from carrying out the same procedure with each chapter, as follows:

1. Try to read the chapter in one sitting. As you do this, bear in mind any advice given in the *Points to Consider* section.
2. Study the flow diagram at the end of the chapter, ensuring that you understand the general 'shape' of what you have just read.
3. Read the *Working on...* section and decide what further work you need to do on the chapter. In particularly important sections of the book, this is likely to involve reading the chapter a second time and stopping at each heading and sub-heading to think about (and probably to write a summary of) what you have just read.
4. Attempt the *Source-based questions* section. It will sometimes be sufficient to think through your answers, but additional understanding will often be gained by forcing yourself to write them down.

When you have finished the main chapters of the book, study the 'Further Reading' section and decide what additional reading (if any) you will do on the topic.

This book has been designed to help make your studies both enjoyable and successful. If you can think of ways in which this could have been done more effectively, please contact us. In the meantime, we hope that you will gain greatly from your study of History.

Keith Randell & Robert Pearce

1 Introduction

POINTS TO CONSIDER

This chapter is about the achievements and influence of the Prussian statesman Otto von Bismarck. It begins by considering his contribution to the unification of Germany and his relationship with the first kaisers of the new Imperial Germany – Wilhelm I, Frederick III and Wilhelm II. The latter part of the chapter then considers his legacy, the extent to which his policies continued to influence German political, economic and military developments after his resignation in 1890.

KEY DATES

1806 End of the Holy Roman Empire
1834 The establishment of the *Zollverein*
1864 Prussia at war with Denmark
1866 Austrio-Prussian War
1870 Franco-Prussian War
1871 Wilhelm proclaimed Emperor of Germany
Bismarck, Chancellor of Germany
Imperial constitution introduced
1873 Start of the *Kulturkampf*
1888 Frederick III, Emperor of Germany
Wilhelm II, Emperor of Germany
1890 Bismarck resigned as Chancellor

1 Unification and Bismarck's Germany

KEY ISSUE To what extent was Bismarck responsible for bringing about the unification of Germany and deciding the new Empire's policies?

Before 1806, central Europe, including the country that is modern day Germany, was made up of some 400 states and was known as the Holy Roman Empire. Although the states had much in common and the language of the people was mainly German, each had its own ruler – king, prince, duke, landgrave or elector – and each jealously guarded its independence. In 1806, the Holy Roman Empire came to an end and nine years later, the number of German states was reduced to 39. They were formed into a loose grouping called the German Confederation. During the years that followed, the two most powerful states, Prussia and Austria, competed for the leadership of the Confederation. In 1834, Prussia gained an advantage by setting up a free trade area or *Zollverein*. Afterwards, Prussia continued to gain the upper hand and, under the leadership of Otto von Bismarck, worked to exclude Austria from German affairs and to achieve the unification of the other German states under Prussian leadership. Bismarck famously warned that this would not be brought about 'by speeches and the resolutions of majorities but by blood and iron.' Following a series of wars fought in 1864, 1866 and 1870 Bismarck finally achieved his aim and in January 1871, King Wilhelm of Prussia was proclaimed Emperor of Germany. During the next twenty years Bismarck controlled German affairs and he saw to it that his country developed into a powerful industrial nation protected by a well-equipped and modern army. But he did not have things all his own way and he had to deal with groups who were dissatisfied with his nationalistic German State. In 1873, he declared a 'war for civilisation' or *Kulturkampf* against the Roman Catholic Church and later he took measures to reduce the influence of the German socialists and their political party, the Social Democratic Party. Bismarck got on well with Kaiser Wilhelm I who largely let him have his own way. In 1888, the old Kaiser died and the Chancellor's relationship with his son and successor, Frederick III, was less friendly. Within a year, the new Kaiser had also died to be succeeded by his son, the twenty-nine year old Wilhelm II. Differences of opinion between the new Kaiser and his Chancellor led to Bismarck's resignation in 1890. Let us now examine the extent to which Imperial Germany remained influenced by Bismarck's policies and consider the nature and problems of the imperial constitution he had introduced earlier in 1871.

2 The Legacy of Bismarck

Wilhelm I, King of Prussia (1861–88) and Emperor of Germany (1871–88), once said about his relationship with Bismarck: 'It isn't easy to be an emperor under a chancellor like this one'. However, in spite of the heartache and frustration implied by this comment, Bismarck and his sovereign worked together most effectively for just over a quarter of a century. Such an understanding did not prove possible with the Emperor's son Frederick III (1888) and even less so with his grandson, Wilhelm II (1888–1918), after his accession to the throne in June 1888. In less than two years the two men had fallen out on both a personal and a political level, and on 18 March 1890 Bismarck offered his resignation. Wilhelm II gladly accepted it. Few contemporaries in Germany regretted Bismarck's fall from favour. The 'Iron Chancellor', as he was known, had successfully forged the unification of Germany out of a collection of independent and self-governing states and had then managed the new nation's affairs for nearly twenty years, by which time Germany had developed into the most powerful state on mainland Europe. Even

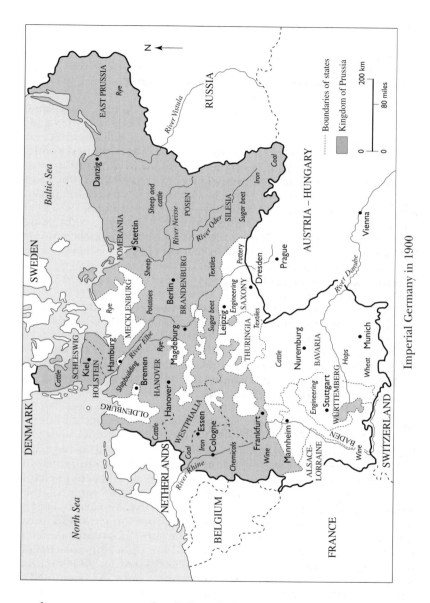

Imperial Germany in 1900

so, there were many who believed that Bismarck had outlived his usefulness and that the young Kaiser offered a new course that was preferable. From the outset, Bismarck's legacy was viewed by many as a mixed blessing.

3 Bismarck's Constitution

> **KEY ISSUE** What were Bismarck's main aims when he framed the German constitution in 1871?

The constitution of the German Empire had been drawn up by Bismarck in 1871 and was most unusual. It has been said that it 'did not fit easily into any category known to the political scientists', and that it was an uneasy settlement between those with opposed political views and the military might of Prussia. Bismarck's attempt to reach agreement between such differing ideas created problems which were not originally apparent but which gradually emerged with the passing of time. The Reich consisted of 25 sovereign states. These were made up of four kingdoms, six grand duchies, four duchies, eight principalities, three free cities and the territory of Alsace-Lorraine annexed in 1871 after the war with France.

a) The dominance of Prussia

In theory, the states came together voluntarily and enjoyed equal status. However, in reality there was no disguising the dominant role of Prussia. Prussia provided two-thirds of the territory of Imperial Germany, the German *Reich,* and as King of Prussia, Wilhelm II was automatically Emperor or *Kaiser* of Germany. In this capacity he enjoyed great authority as of right: he had the final word over the direction of Germany's foreign policy. He was commander-in-chief of all armed forces within the Empire both in peace and war. In addition, he alone could appoint and dismiss the Chancellor and the state secretaries who made up the imperial government. Such were the powers available to Wilhelm II, if he had the will to use them. Bismarck's concession to federalism, the idea that whilst policies of national importance were decided by the central government, in domestic matters the individual states still retained some of their former independence, was the creation of the *Bundesrat* (Federal Council). It consisted of 58 representatives from the various state governments and was, at least in theory, the most important decision-making body in the Empire. It alone had the right to make changes to the constitution and its agreement was required for all legislation. Even so, the influence of Prussia was greatest since it was entitled to 17 of the seats in the *Bundesrat*. This was important since the opposition of just 14 votes was sufficient to reject any military or constitutional issue. This meant that Prussia was able to guarantee its privileged position within the political structure of the Empire.

However, it is all too easy to underestimate the powers of the various states individually. Although the imperial government had complete control over foreign policy and defence, currency, banking, and matters relating to trade, responsibility for education, justice and health remained in the hands of the states. Most significantly, only the states could raise direct taxes, that is taxes on income. The imperial government was prohibited from levying a national income tax and was therefore dependent upon indirect taxes such as customs duties and taxes on goods and services. This was of great importance, since it limited the expenditure of the imperial government.

b) The role of the *Reichstag*

Another major section of Bismarck's constitution related to the *Reichstag* (the Imperial Parliament), which was elected directly by universal suffrage and secret ballot. However, this apparent concession to liberal democracy was in reality limited in scope. For, although Bismarck always desired the co-operation of the *Reichstag* in the passage of legislation, he went to considerable lengths to make sure that even governments with majorities did not have the same privileges and status as those enjoyed in Britain by House of Commons at the end of the nineteenth century. The *Reichstag* was not permitted to introduce legislation of its own but could only discuss and agree those proposals put forward by the *Bundesrat* and the imperial government. Above all, the imperial government was not accountable to it. The *Reichstag* was therefore a representative assembly without real power which, of course, was as Bismarck intended.

The implications of these aspects of the German constitution were to give rise to causes for concern long after Bismarck's day. Above all, it had aimed to ensure the position and power of Bismarck himself and to preserve the privileges of Prussia and its ruling class by a system of checks and balances. Yet, even with Bismarck still at the helm there were occasions when political disagreements led to deadlocks during which government came to a standstill. It was already obvious that the power structure was confused and unclear. From 1888 this situation had been worsened by the accession of an emperor who was no longer prepared to sit on the sidelines. Only then did the weakness of the chancellor's position reveal itself. The chancellor was solely responsible to the emperor and as Wilhelm II wished to exert a more personal rule than his father or grandfather, this was bound to lead to confusion in government unless both emperor and chancellor showed a mutual respect and shared a common political outlook.

In 1890 such problems would not have been impossible to overcome if only the political system had shown a degree of flexibility. However, the firmly fixed framework of Bismarck's constitution proved to be a major weakness. There was only very limited scope for adjusting to changing circumstances at a time when important major changes were taking place. Germany in the second half of the nineteenth century was in the middle of a period of rapid social and economic change. It had experienced a massive industrial progress in the

1850s and 1860s, and, in spite of the fact that this had slowed after 1873, there is no doubt that by 1890 two major landmarks had been achieved. Firstly, Germany had changed from being a mainly agricultural country to being a modern industrial state; secondly, it had surpassed all its economic rivals on the continent of Europe, though it had not yet overtaken Great Britain. The social consequences of these economic changes were enormous. Not only was the traditional structure of society altered, but also millions of ordinary Germans had to come to terms with dramatic changes in their lifestyle. These in turn affected traditional patterns of behaviour and ties of loyalty. Such was the nature of the legacy of Bismarck in 1890, when the young Wilhelm II decided to assume the personal rule of his empire.

Summary Diagram
The Legacy of Bismarck

Constitution of 1871	Economic growth	Military might
Ensured the continued power of the Kaiser, the Chancellor and the Prussian ruling class	Massive economic development that turned Imperial Germany into a modern industrial state	The security of Imperial Germany was guaranteed by a modern and well-equipped army based on Prussian military traditions

Working on Chapter I

This introductory chapter should have enabled you to identify the main historical issues and debates raised by this period of history and also to familiarise yourself with the historical background. If you have already studied nineteenth century German history, the chapter should have presented no problems at all. Indeed, if this is your situation, it would probably be best for you to look back over your previous notes and then only to jot down anything from this chapter that seems particularly unfamiliar to you.

However, if modern German history is a new historical topic for you, then you will probably need to read this chapter for a second time in order to try to understand as much of it as you can. But remember, this chapter is quite demanding and you will probably find some of the ideas difficult to grasp. Don't worry. It is only intended to highlight some of the key issues you will be considering in the rest of the book. If you manage to keep some of these in mind as you work on the following chapters, it will help you when we come to our concluding chapter.

Answering source-based questions on Chapter I

In answering source-based questions it is important that your answers are based on information provided in the source. Only use your own background information if you are invited to do so. If you are asked to evaluate the source, that is explain how useful it is to a historian, it is necessary to consider the accuracy and reliability of the source and explain its shortcomings. Is it biased or limited in its content? If so, what essential detail has been over-looked?

I. Read the following source carefully and then answer the questions based on it.

1 If you wish to make the selection of cabinet ministers the prerogative of the Emperor and not be controlled by parliament... there shall be a clear statement in the constitution that the Emperor has the responsibility to select the ministers... He shall appoint and dismiss them...
5 Thus, because the power of appointment and dismissal belongs to the Emperor, the ministers depend upon the favour of the Emperor and they are not controlled by the opinions of the people... Thus is based the Prussian Constitution which we must copy... Article 109 of the Prussian Constitution agrees that if the government and parliament
10 cannot agree on the annual budget, the budget of the previous year remains effective. This provision is most important because it sustains administrative power... If we wish to form a cabinet with no regard for parliament on the model of Prussia, we must copy the tax arrangements of that country... I believe these measures are necessary to... protect
15 the happiness of the nation forever.

(A Japanese official recommends the Prussian constitution to his Emperor on returning from a visit to that country in 1881.)

a) What is meant by i) 'the prerogative of the Emperor' and ii) 'it sustains administrative power'? (2 × 2 = 4 marks)

b) According to the source, for what reasons is the Japanese official recommending the Prussian Constitution to his Emperor? (6 marks)

c) How useful is the source to an understanding of the Prussian Constitution? (In your answer you are advised to use your own relevant background knowledge as well as information derived from the source.) (10 marks)

Some interpretation questions require you to evaluate a quotation. In addition to reaching conclusions about value and accuracy of the quotation, it is necessary to consider the attribution, in other words, to consider the reliability of the author. Many authors will be academics who have studied the subject in depth and will have the benefit of hindsight and subsequent research. However, this does not automatically prevent them being biased or putting forward an unconvincing interpretation. Certainly, their accuracy cannot always be guaranteed.

Essay-type questions on Chapter 1

1. 'Bismarck's constitution was no more than a sham. Its basic aim was the retention of power.' (Dudley Woodget, a modern British historian, in *Europe 1789–1914*.)

   How valid is this interpretation of Bismarck's constitution?

The Structure of Imperial Germany, 1890–1914

POINTS TO CONSIDER

At the height of the diplomatic crisis in July 1914 that eventually led to the First World War, the Austrian foreign minister asked: 'Who actually rules in Berlin?' It was a fair question for it neatly sums up the key issues facing historians of Imperial Germany. In this chapter we will examine the power structure of the *Kaiserreich*. We will also consider who exerted the greatest influence on policy and the aims of that leadership. The chapter concludes by looking at the major political, social and economic forces that affected life of Imperial Germany.

1 Economic and Social Change

> **KEY ISSUE** What were the reasons for Germany's rapid growth into a major industrial nation?

a) The growth of the German economy

When Wilhelm II came to the throne in 1888, the German economy had already completed what economic historians call a 'take-off' into sustained economic growth. By 1890, further economic development had led to the dominance of industry over agriculture. In spite of slumps in the economy in 1891 and 1901, the years 1890 to 1914 were to witness another period of economic expansion and industrial growth. This was brought about partly by continued increases in production in those industries associated with the first stages of industrialisation – coal, iron, heavy engineering and textiles – and partly because the economy expanded into other areas of manufacture – steel, chemicals and electronics (see the table on pages 10–11). By 1914 Germany had become Europe's industrial superpower. It had already exceeded Britain's level of iron and steel production and had nearly caught up with that country's coal production. It was by far the largest manufacturer of cotton cloth on the continent. However, what really marked out the German economy in the 25 years before the First World War was the expansion of the newer industries. German steel production increased nearly nine-fold in this period and by 1914 German output was double that of Britain. Even more impressive was the emergence of the electrical, chemical and motor construction industries. Two German firms, AEG and Siemens, came to dominate the world market to such an extent that by 1913 it is reckoned that nearly 50 per cent of the world's electrical products originated from Germany. It was a similar story in the chemicals industry, where the extraction of potash and potassium salts massively increased the availability of fertilisers, and where research and development in the manufacture of chemicals gave Germany a world lead in the preparation of dyes and pharmaceutical products.

The Development of the German Economy

1 Population (in millions)

Year	Total	Per Cent in Towns over 2,000
1871	41.1	36.1
1880	42.2	41.4
1890	49.4	42.5
1900	56.4	54.4
1910	64.9	60.0

2 Output of Heavy Industry (in millions of tonnes)
(a) Coal

Year	Germany	UK
1871	37.7	119.2
1880	59.1	149.3
1890	89.2	184.5
1900	149.5	228.8
1910	222.2	268.7

(b) Steel

Year	Germany	UK
1871	0.14	0.41
1880	0.69	1.32
1890	2.13	3.64
1900	6.46	4.98
1910	13.10	6.48

3 Index of Industrial Production (1913 = 100)

Year	
1871	21.0
1880	49.4
1890	57.3
1900	61.0
1910	86.0
1913	100.0

4 Balance of Payments (in millions of marks)

Year	Imports	Exports	Visible Balance	Invisible Balance	Overall Balance
1880	2,814	2,923	+109	+168	+277
1890	4,162	3,335	−827	+1,249	+422
1900	5,769	4,611	−1,158	+1,566	+408
1910	8,927	7,475	−1,452	+2,211	+759

Visible balance refers to the payment and receipts for the import and export of goods; invisible balance refers to the payment and receipts for the import and export for services such as banking, insurance and shipping.

5 Structure of Labour Force (in millions of workers)

Sector	1875	1895	1913
Agriculture	9.23	9.79	10.7
Mining	0.29	0.43	0.86
Industry	5.15	7.52	10.86
Transport	0.35	0.62	1.17
Commerce/Banking	1.12	1.97	3.47
Hotels/Domestic	1.49	1.57	1.54
Defence	0.43	0.61	0.86
Other	0.59	0.89	1.49
Total	18.64	23.40	30.97

The economic picture these figures present seems clear-cut. Germany had rapidly built on its earlier foundations and by 1914 had grown into the most powerful industrial economy on the European continent, with a share of world trade which rivalled that of Britain and its Empire. How and why did this come about?

Firstly, Germany's population continued to grow rapidly. There were one-third more Germans in 1910 than there had been in 1890.

This provided both the market and the labour force for an expanding economy. Moreover, the balance of the population was towards the younger generations and this made it easier for workers to move from job to job and adapt to new skills. Both were essential in the change-over to a more advanced level of economic production. The availability of raw materials was also important and Germany had an abundance of natural resources. There was coal from the Ruhr, Saar Basin and Silesia; iron-ore from Alsace-Lorraine and the Ruhr and potash from Alsace-Lorraine. Thus, to a large extent, the huge demand for energy, iron-steel products and chemicals could be met from domestic supplies instead of depending on imports. This was a huge benefit for the balance of payments – the difference in the total payments received from other countries for exports compared with the amounts paid to them for imports. Other geographical advantages included navigable rivers, such as the Rhine and the Elbe, and the broad flat northern plain that was well suited to the construction of railways. To such natural advantages must be added skills and efficiency of the German people. Germany had probably the best elementary education system in the world. Even more importantly, its institutes of higher education not only provided for the traditional scholar, but also made increasing provision for those with technical skills.

2 The German Banking System and the Development of Cartels

> **KEY ISSUE** Why were cartels so important to the development of the German economy?

Another area of expertise was the German banking system that had traditionally played such an important role in trade and industry. In the last decade of the century the banking system expanded enormously. Free from any kind of state control, German banks pursued an adventurous policy of providing generous long-term loans. This in turn led the big banks to become directly involved in industrial research and development, as their own representatives were often invited on to the boards of directors of firms. This helped to create a close partnership between the banking and commercial sectors of the economy. The banks also contributed to the development of a distinctly German feature of industrialisation, the growth of cartels. A cartel is a type of organisation that limits the number of firms producing a product. It aims to restrict the amount produced and so keep up the price of the product. The firms that are part of the cartel agree to a code of conduct that is rigidly enforced. In reality, cartels simply create a monopoly situation. In Britain and the USA the idea of a group of businessmen combining together to control prices, production levels and marketing was frowned upon as against the spirit of free enterprise. In Germany they were accepted and legally protected. Indeed, the state even encouraged their development. Since they restricted competition and encouraged development and investment, especially important at times of recession, they were viewed as a sensible means of taking advantage of the benefits of large-scale production and achieving economies of scale. According to a government investigation, by 1905, 366 cartels existed compared to only 90 in 1885. In effect, whole areas of German industry had been 'cartelised'. To many at that time, the cartels were typical of the efficient large-scale and productive nature of the German economy. In recent decades, economic historians have questioned the extent to which cartels did really benefit the German economy since, by restricting the entry of new manufacturers, they reduced competition and maintained artificially high prices.

3 German Society

> **KEY ISSUE** What were the main divisions within German society during the Second Empire?

In simple terms, the impact of this rapid change into an industrial power meant that millions of ordinary Germans were forced to come to terms with changes in their way of life. Admittedly, in some of the more rural areas, such as much of Bavaria and almost all of Pomerania, time stood still, but few could escape the consequences of change. The difficulty for the historian is trying to draw some meaningful conclusions about the social effects of these changes without being too general. Such difficulties are even more noticeable in German social history. Here, any attempt to consider the make-up of the German people on the basis of class is complicated by the existence of other lines of division such as those of religion and regional and national identity.

Bismarck may have unified Germany but religious and nationalist feelings were still very powerful influences that cut across all classes of society. This is most clearly shown in religion by the solidity of the vote for the Catholic Centre Party (see page 24), especially in Bavaria and the Rhineland, and the success of Catholic trade unions in providing an alternative to the socialist trade unions. It is also significant that over ten per cent of the *Reichstag*'s seats continued to be won by deputies supporting one of the minority nationalist groupings – Poles, Danes and French.

Bearing in mind these important factors, what then were the main social features of Kaiser Wilhelm's or Wilhelmine Germany? Surprisingly, in spite of the economic changes, German society seems to have remained divided along traditional class lines. What

movement there was tended to be within a class rather than movement between the different classes. Divisions were maintained and it
was difficult to achieve higher social status simply on the grounds of
wealth or expertise. Thus, as one historian has written, 'the large
majority of working class sons did not leave their class; the majority of
the lower middle class continued to come from the lower middle
class.' The prejudices of class, religion and race acted as very effective
barriers to the lessening of class differences. This was seen in the education system, the professions, the business world, and most promi-
nently at the top levels of society, where the higher ranks of the civil
service and the army remained predominantly the preserve of the
nobility.

The landed nobility or *Junkers* continued to be an extremely powerful force in society. In economic terms many in this class were beginning to experience less prosperous times. Agriculture was in relative
decline, as measured against industry, and those landowners who
failed to modernise their production methods or who did not adapt
to changing market conditions were likely to find their financial position under threat. Yet the nobility still regarded their privileged
social status as not only essential to maintaining the traditions and
values of German society, but also as a right and proper reflection of
their social superiority built up over many generations. The greatest
threat to the nobility's supremacy came from the wealthy new industrialists. However, most research suggests that successful German businessmen were willing to purchase privileges and to flaunt their wealth
in an attempt to copy the *Junkers* rather than to replace them. After
all, the policies and the actions of the National Liberals (see page 24)
who were in the main representatives of business and industry
became increasingly conservative in their outlook and supportive of
the existing system.

The middle ranks of the middle class were also becoming more
numerous. Professional and clerical workers in industry, education
and the bureaucracy were in great demand for their scientific, technical or administrative skills. Even so, here too the tendency was to try
to keep things as they were rather than to seek change. Teachers, civil
servants and others employed in the public services, for example,
were classified as *Beamte* or state officials, and in return for accepting
the state's strict regulations of employment, they were guaranteed
rights of employment and certain privileges, such as pensions. This
status was highly cherished and widely respected.

However, for the old *Mittelstand*, the lower-middle class of skilled
workers and small traders, times were not so good. The problems they
faced went a lot deeper than merely coping when times were difficult.
The *Mittelstand* found itself squeezed between the more powerful
workers who had formed trade unions and the larger, more productive enterprises of big business. As a result, resentment led many in
this class to regard the old times, before the age of industrialisation,

as a golden bygone era. It also led to a simple and unrealistic belief that their fears might be overcome by supporting the views and solutions offered by the extreme right in politics.

At the bottom of the social pyramid was the mass of the population who made up the labouring classes in both the towns and countryside. For the smallholders and landless labourers life was particularly difficult. The economic problems of agriculture at this time combined with the growth in population meant that it was difficult to make farming pay. In the south and west of Germany, where the land was mainly farmed as smallholdings, families were often forced to divide the land between their children who then combined farming with other part-time occupations. In the east, the labourers on the estates of the aristocratic and landed *Junkers* had little option but to accept wage cuts. Not surprisingly, to many on the land the prospect of industrial employment with the prospect of regular work and wages seemed an attractive option. This meant that the drift of rural workers to the cities continued.

However, life in the industrial regions had its own problems. Whilst employment rates were very good and unemployment only went above three per cent in one year between 1900 and 1914, and the average wage increased by 25 per cent between 1895 and 1913, living and working conditions remained dismally poor. Thus, for most working people, life was divided between long hours in often unhealthy workplaces and the cold cramped accommodation in the insanitary houses which were their homes. As a leading historian has put it: 'Some 30 per cent of all family households in this prosperous Second Empire lived in destitution and abject misery'.

There is little doubt therefore that the rapid pace of economic change in Imperial Germany had an important effect upon the stability of an already mixed society. Whilst the traditional social ties and values were still very strong, economic progress inevitably led to rivalry, tensions and disorder. It was the problem of balancing the old with the new, of accommodating the various groups in German society which the political system somehow had to manage.

4 The Political System

> **KEY ISSUE** How significant was the role of the Kaiser in the politics of Imperial Germany?

a) The Emperor and his court

Whether one should start to study the political system of Imperial Germany with a consideration of the role of the kaiser is an issue of historical debate in itself. Many historians would strongly argue that such an approach implies an excessively 'personalistic' approach by which they mean that the study becomes too closely identified with one individual. This is certainly not the intended purpose of starting this section by discussing the emperor and his court. It is simply a recognition of the fact that the role of kaiser is one of the most important issues in historical debate about the *Kaiserreich*.

WILHELM II (BORN 1859, DIED 1941) — *-Profile-*

1859	born in Berlin. His father was the eldest son of the King of Prussia and his mother was the eldest daughter of Queen Victoria.
1860	made his first visit to Britain.
1862	attended the wedding of his uncle, the future Edward VII, and Princess Alexandra of Denmark.
1869	commissioned as a second lieutenant in the Pomeranian Regiment.
1878	began his studies at the University of Bonn.
1881	married Princess Augusta-Victoria of Schleswig-Holstein.
1888	became Crown Prince following the death of his grandfather and then became Kaiser on the death of his father.
1890	dismissed his Chancellor, Otto von Bismarck.
1914	policies and attitude contributed to the outbreak of war in 1914.
1915	began to be overshadowed by the military leadership.
1918	abdicated and fled to Holland. Spent the rest of his life living in exile at Doorn.
1940	declined an offer from Hitler to return and live as a private citizen.
1941	died.

He was born with a deformed arm and there has been much speculation about the possible psychological effects that this had upon his character. He was educated at home and later at the University of Bonn. During his adolescent years, he disapproved of the liberal sympathies of his parents and this led to a strained relationship. Gradually they grew apart.

He was an arrogant and self-opinionated man. Soon after he became Kaiser in 1888 he clashed with his Chancellor, Otto von Bismarck, and he dismissed him in 1890. He was badly served by subsequent chancellors and became increasingly isolated. With the intention of strengthening Germany's position in Europe, he followed an increasingly adventurous foreign policy that contributed significantly to the outbreak of a European war in 1914.

During this time he made a number of ill-advised policy decisions and there were those who began to question his mental state.

During the course of the war, his influence rapidly declined and he was forced to play a subordinate role to Germany's military leaders Hindenburg and Ludendorff. Forced to abdicate in 1918, he fled to Holland and there made his home for the next twenty years. The Allied leaders made a request that he be tried as a war criminal but this was rejected by the Dutch authorities. During the early years of the Second World War, he was offered asylum in both Britain and Germany but these he declined.

Basically, Wilhelm II lacked personal charisma and leadership qualities. He failed to appreciate the changes that were happening in Germany and more generally in Europe. At home, he opposed parliamentary rule; abroad he supported adventurous and therefore dangerous foreign policies. During the First World War, he just lost control of events. The historian B.J. Elliott says of him 'he was simply not big enough for his role in life'. Winston Churchill was kinder when he said, 'It was not his fault. It was his fate'.

b) The Kaiser's personality

There is still much disagreement among historians about the true nature of the personality of Wilhelm II. He was intelligent and at times an extremely charming man. He had a broad range of interests and took great pride in his country and ancestry. However, his understanding of issues was usually slight and distorted by his own personal prejudices. Above all, he was very sensitive to criticism and so taken up by his own self-importance that his moods and behaviour were liable to wild fluctuations. His closest friend, Prinz Philipp zu Ellensburg, whilst on a North Sea cruise with his sovereign in 1900, expressed his concern in correspondence with Bernhard von Bülow, later to become chancellor:

1 'H.M. is no longer in control of himself when He is seized by rage. I regard the situation as highly dangerous and am at a loss to know what to do ... These things cut me to the quick. I have had so much faith in the Kaiser's abilities – and in the passage of time! – Now both have
5 failed, and one sees a person suffering whom one loves dearly but cannot help.'

Subsequent profiles have suggested that the Kaiser's behaviour can be seen as symptoms of insanity, megalomania (delusions about his own greatness) and sadism (pleasure in inflicting pain on others). More recently, it has been suggested that he was narcissistic (showed signs of excessive self-love), a repressed homosexual and suffered from a mental condition which revealed itself in his irrational behaviour. It is difficult to be sure about any of these claims, but the general opinion now is that Wilhelm II, if not insane, was at least deeply disturbed. However, besides attempting to draw conclusions about Wilhelm the man, the historian must also try to decide the extent to which Wilhelm's personality actually shaped the history of Imperial Germany.

Wilhelm II once boasted that he had never read the German constitution. Bearing in mind the complications of Bismarck's constitutional plans, his failure to do so was perhaps understandable. However, the story gives an interesting insight into the outlook of Germany's sovereign. He had no doubts about his position. He considered himself to be all-powerful, with his authority based on the divine right of kings. He was accountable to God alone. He was also of the Hohenzollern dynasty of kings and, as such, was a warrior king who led and commanded his people militarily. In 1891 he spoke to some new recruits as follows:

1   Recruits! You have sworn Me allegiance. That, children of My Guard, means that you are now My soldiers. You have given yourselves over to Me body and soul. There is only one enemy for you and that is My enemy. With the present Socialist agitation, it may be that I shall order
5   you to shoot down your own families, your brothers, yes, your parents – which may God forbid – but then too you must follow my orders without murmur.

c) The Kaiser's personal rule

Of course, it is true that the constitution did indeed grant the emperor extensive powers, but his ignorance of its other aspects was a dangerous misunderstanding and self-deception. His desire to establish 'personal rule' was made possible by his total control over appointments to the imperial government. He also enjoyed the same right over the government of Prussia. Bismarck had at least given the system a degree of unity and direction, but the Kaiser possessed neither the character nor the ability of his former chancellor and his leadership amounted to little more than flights of fancy and blundering interventions. This situation was allowed to continue because he made all the important appointments. By this means the Kaiser was able to surround himself at court and in government with men who were prepared to bolster his own high opinion of himself by sympathising with his views. In this sense it is perhaps possible to speak of the Kaiser's 'personal rule'.

This view of the Kaiser's 'personal rule' as a system of government centred on the imperial court has been most strongly argued by the historian John Röhl. Following extensive research, especially amongst the private letters of leading figures of that time, he has built up a portrait of the Kaiser to support his theories regarding the political situation at that time. He concludes that the characteristics of the Kaiser's personality do suggest that he was a mentally unbalanced character. The Kaiser's usual mood generally showed signs of mental illness and on occasions it turned into uncontrollable rage. Röhl goes on to argue that this neurotic character, flattered and charmed by an inner circle of friends, advisers and military officers, created a situation in which he gained control over all other sources of power.

At the centre of this system were the two mutual friends, Count Philip Eulenburg and Prince Bernhard von Bülow. Eulenburg and the Kaiser were undoubtedly very close. The Kaiser spoke of him as his only 'bosom friend', and Eulenburg 'loved [the Kaiser] above everything else'. Bülow's relationship with the Kaiser was also a close one. He was an insincere flatterer who tailored his letters and conversations to satisfy Wilhelm. This was a successful strategy and in the end he achieved his aim and became chancellor. In 1898 he wrote to Eulenburg in apparently unambiguous terms:

1   I grow fonder and fonder of the Kaiser. He is so important!! Together with the Great King and the Great Elector he is by far the most important Hohenzollern ever to have lived. In a way I have never before seen he combines genius – the most authentic and original genius – with the
5   clearest *bon sens* (good sense). His vivid imagination lifts me like an eagle high above petty detail, yet he can judge soberly what is or is not possible and attainable. And what vitality! What a memory! How quick and sure his understanding! In the Crown Council this morning I was completely overwhelmed!

Röhl has placed Wilhelm's personality at the very centre of his interpretation of Imperial Germany. However, before looking at other alternative sources of power and influence, it is worth bearing in mind several points. The Kaiser's grasp of politics was limited. He was essentially a lazy and pleasure-seeking man. He was never able to settle down to the regular routine required of government and administration. He much preferred to spend his time playing the social and ceremonial roles of a monarch. He liked to travel and to take part in military manoeuvres and was absent from Berlin for long periods. The Kaiser may have appeared and behaved as an all-powerful autocrat. Was his claim that 'there is only one Ruler in the Reich and I am he' just another example of his own delusion of power? As always, it is important that the history student distinguishes between the images of the time and what was historically discovered to be true.

d) The Kaiser's relationship with his Chancellors

German Chancellors 1890–1917

1890–1894	Count Leo von Caprivi
1894–1900	Prince Chlodwig Hohenlohe-Schillingfurst
1900–1909	Prince Bernhard von Bülow
1909–1917	Theobald von Bethmann-Hollweg

If Wilhelm II was incapable of governing the country alone, the responsibility first fell upon his appointed chancellor. However, none of Bismarck's successors were able to take up the mantle of leadership with any kind of real authority and conviction. Why was this?

The short-lived chancellorship of Count Leo von Caprivi (1890–4) is proof enough that good intentions, integrity and a friendly approach were not sufficient in the political environment of Wilhelmine Germany. He was appointed in 1890 by Wilhelm II in order to restore legal recognition to the Germany socialist party. The party had earlier been outlawed under Bismarck. Then in 1894 Caprivi felt obliged to resign when his master demanded the drafting of a Subversion Bill that was aimed against the very same party! He was succeeded by Prince Hohenlohe-Schillingfurst (1894–1900), an elderly Bavarian aristocrat. His reputation for indecision and long windedness offered exactly the kind of weak leadership that allowed others to exercise influence. Hohenlohe-Schillingfurst was soon reduced to little more than a figure-head, so that even before Bülow became chancellor (1900–9) the latter had come to exert the more powerful political influence as foreign minister (1897–1900). In December 1897 Bülow wrote to Eulenburg:

1 I am putting the main emphasis on foreign policy... Only a successful
   foreign policy can help to reconcile, pacify, rally, unite. Its preconditions
   are of course, caution, patience, tact, reflection... It is not a good idea
   to sound a victory fanfare before the definitive victory, excessive sabre-
5 rattling annoys without frightening.

Another political observer, the Württemberg ambassador, commented on Bülow's political tactics in slightly different terms:

1 I alone have reason to assume that Herr von Bülow, in refraining from
   closer contact with the individual Reichstag parties, is pursuing a well-con-
   sidered intention not to become involved in the economic and social questions of the state, but, as far as possible, to limit himself and to concentrate
5 on his department of foreign policy – partly because this alone already lays
   total claim to his physical and mental powers, partly too in order not to
   eclipse completely the Reich chancellor – last not least, in case he himself
   is called upon to take his place, in order to keep himself intact vis-à-vis the
   parliamentary parties and not use himself up prematurely.

BERNHARD VON BÜLOW (1849–1920)

-Profile-

1849 born in Klein-Flottbeck
1870 served in Prussian army during Franco-Prussian War
1873 entered the diplomatic service
1897 appointed foreign secretary
1900 chancellor of Imperial Germany
1908 the *Daily Telegraph* affair
1909 resigned and appointed ambassador to Italy
1915 retired from public life
1920 died

Bülow was a scheming politician by nature who found that he was able to manipulate the Kaiser to further his own position. In domestic policy, he had few sound ideas. Whilst his foreign policy aimed to win the friendship of Britain, he alienated France, at the time of the Moroccan crisis (1905), and Russia, as a result of the Bosnian crisis (1908). He was largely responsible for strengthening the ties between Britain, France and Russia that led to the Triple Entente. In 1909, he was forced to resign when he failed to give the Kaiser adequate support following Wilhelm's indiscreet interview with the *Daily Telegraph*. Later, as ambassador to Italy, he failed to prevent that country entering the First World War on the side of the Allies. It is said that 'his career was a casualty of his own ambition'. After his retirement, he sought to redeem himself by writing an autobiography that revealed the political corruption and personal jealousies that existed within the German government.

A year later Bülow did become chancellor and for nearly a decade he successfully combined the roles of courtier and chancellor. He kept the affection and trust of the Kaiser and he effectively handled the *Reichstag*. However, Bülow's domination from 1897–1909 should not be mistaken for genuine authority and purpose. Bülow was a manipulator, whose main concern was to further himself. He thought that this could best be achieved by pandering to the emperor. Eventually, when he failed to show sufficient loyalty to the Kaiser during the '*Daily Telegraph* affair', he lost that all important prop and his removal soon followed. Germany's last chancellor before the First World War was Theobald von Bethmann-Hollweg (1909–17), a hard-working and well-meaning bureaucrat, whose virtues were not really suited to the demands of the situation. At a time of growing international tension between the great powers in Europe his lack of experience in foreign affairs and his ignorance of military issues were highly significant.

THEOBALD BETHMANN-HOLLWEG (1856–1921)

-Profile-

1856 born in Howenfinow, Brandenburg
1905 appointed Prussian Minister for the Interior
1909 replaced Bulow as Imperial Chancellor
1914 played a major role in events leading to the First World War
1917 opposed unrestricted submarine warfare and wanted to negotiate for peace
1917 forced to resign
1921 died

When appointed Imperial Chancellor in 1909, Bethmann-Hollweg was relatively inexperienced in political matters. He was an earnest and conscientious man but he lacked a dominant personality. As a result he failed to get a number of domestic reforms passed by the *Reichstag*. He is best remembered for his part in the events leading to the First World War (see pages 52–4). It was he who, in 1914, famously referred to the treaty by which Britain had agreed to guarantee Belgian neutrality as 'a scrap of paper'. Although he played a major part in the events leading to the First World War, he never expected it to escalate into a major European conflict. It is claimed that he hoped that a limited war would divert opposition to his economic policies. It had been claimed that 'he was a weak politician who stumbled into war through sheer incapacity'. He became deeply unpopular with both conservatives and liberals in the *Reichstag* as well as the military and was forced to resign from office in 1917. In the 1960s, much controversy was caused when Fritz Fisher published *Grif nach der Weltmacht* in which he accused Bethmann-Hollweg of consciously trying to achieve German domination of Europe (see pages 35–6).

Thus, it is clear that Germany's four chancellors in this period were very different in character and background. Yet, none of them was ever really able to dominate the German political scene decisively. It is tempting, therefore, to say that their weaknesses and limited political experience were the reasons for the problems of government. This would be an over-simplification. Imperial Germany got the chancellors it deserved. They were the products of a constitution that made them accountable first and foremost to the Kaiser. Under Wilhelm I this had not mattered since he had consulted Bismarck, but his grandson was determined to be involved in the affairs of state. Political survival for Germany's four chancellors was therefore dependent upon showing loyalty to the Kaiser. This was far from easy when Wilhelm II's personal involvement was often erratic and blundering.

5 The *Reichstag*

> **KEY ISSUE** To what extent did the Kaiser's government depend on the backing of the *Reichstag*?

a) The constitutional position of the *Reichstag*

The problems of government during the years after 1890 were made more difficult by the constitutional position of the *Reichstag*. Bismarck had always been obliged to secure the support of the *Reichstag* for government legislation and by one means or another he had usually managed to achieve that. This task had been made possible by the introduction of laws aimed to curb the socialists in 1878, which had reduced left-wing representation to a handful of seats. After 1890 the balance of power in the *Reichstag* shifted significantly. What were these changes in political representation and what were their implications?

On most issues – there were some important exceptions that we will consider in the next chapter – the Kaiser and his governments could always depend on the backing of the right-wing parties – the *Deutschkonservative Partei*, the *Reichspartei* and the *Nationalliberale Partei*. However the voting strength of these parties was on the decline. In 1887, they gained only 48 per cent of the vote and 55 per cent of the seats in the *Reichstag*. By the time of the election of 1912, the last before the outbreak of the First World War, their share of the vote had further fallen to 26 per cent which gave them only 26 per cent of the seats in the *Reichstag*. During this period, the traditional support for the imperial government was slowly being eroded and this increased the problem of finding majority support to enable the passing of laws. In such a situation the position taken by the liberal and centre parties, the *Deutsche Freisinnige Partei, Zentrumspartie*, the Centre Party, and the *Sozialdemokratische Partei Deutschlands*, became increasingly important.

The Left Liberals (the *Deutsche Freisinnige Partei*), though supportive of the government at times, were generally more critical. However, from 1893 they were divided into at least three factions and were incapable of having a decisive say in the *Reichstag*. The same could not be said of the Centre Party (*Zentrumspartei*). Its importance increased during Bismarck's *Kulturkampf* and afterwards it consistently won between 90 and 110 seats that made it the largest party in the *Reichstag*. A position it continued to hold until the election of 1912. Although it had a religious base, its members embraced a wide range of political views ranging from right-wing conservatism to progressive social reform. Its parliamentary numbers were sufficiently large to ensure that the Centre Party enjoyed an important role in German

THE MAJOR POLITICAL PARTIES REPRESENTED IN THE *REICHSTAG*

SPD Sozialdemokratische Partei Deutschlands. Social Democratic Party. A Marxist party that was closely connected with the trade unions and supported by the working classes. Banned by anti-socialist legislation from 1878–90. Afterwards it grew rapidly.

ZP Zentrumspartei. Centre Party. Formed in 1871 to uphold the interests of the Catholic Church and its members from the threat of Protestant Prussia. Its appeal was therefore denominational rather than class-based. Despite the *Kulturkampf* (Bismarck's anti-Catholic policy of the 1870s) it had become an influential political voice in the *Reichstag*.

DKP Deutschkonservative Partei. German Conservative Party. The party of the land-owning farming community. Its outlook was ultra-conservative and distinctly hostile to the new forces of liberalism. It was especially strong in Prussia.

RP Reichspartei. Free Conservative Party. Conservative in outlook, it was backed by both industrialists and landowners. Its geographical base of support was not so narrow as DKP.

NLP Nationalliberale Partei. National Liberal Party. Traditionally the party of economic and political liberalism. It represented bankers and industrialists and was increasingly conservative in its policy.

DFP Deutsche Freisinnige Partei. German Free Thought Party (Left Liberals). Formed in 1884 following the secession of the more radical elements from the NLP. It attracted support from intellectuals and certain elements of the commercial and professional middle class. In 1893 it split into three and was only reunited in 1910 under the new name of the **FVP, Fortschrittliche Volkspartei**, Progressive People's Party.

Parties representing national minorities. Such parties represented the interests of ethnic minorities living in Germany such as Poles, Danes and the French in Alsace-Lorraine.

Right-wing splinter groups. There were a number of small extreme right-wing conservative parties. They were nationalistic, anti-socialist and often anti-Semitic.

politics. Earlier, even Bismarck had been forced to recognise this. It exploited this position by a sensible, down-to-earth approach to the parliamentary process. At times this led to co-operation and at others to downright opposition. Therefore the Centre Party deputies could not be taken for granted and the imperial government dare not ignore its views.

b) The rise of the Social Democrats

Even more important was the rapid rise of the Social Democrats as a parliamentary force. Strengthened by the years of persecution, and then liberated in 1890 by the removal of the anti-socialist laws, the Social Democratic Party then organised itself into a nationwide mass party. At the Erfurt Congress of 1891, the party adopted a thorough going Marxist programme aimed at overthrowing the Wilhelmine class system. It proved to be a popular policy decision. In 1887 the Social Democrats had polled only 10.1 per cent of the vote and gained 2.8 per cent of the seats (11). In 1912 the figures were 34.8 per cent and 27.7 per cent (110). Yet, although the party had gathered the bulk of the working classes behind its banner, there were very clear divisions within its ranks about how best to achieve its aims. Many of the rank and file, especially the trade unionists, came to believe that a policy of advancing slowly and gradual reform was the best way to create a socialist society. According to this view, parliamentary reforms that improved living and working conditions represented progress towards improving the lot of working people. Traditional Marxists thoroughly disapproved of this approach since it involved co-operation with the *bourgeoisie* – the old and long established and conventional middle classes. Although the differences between the socialists who favoured gradual reform and those who wanted a more revolutionary approach was important. However, up to 1914, it did not greatly weaken the appeal of the Social Democrats. In theory the party remained committed to bringing about revolutionary changes in society, but in practice many of the deputies in the *Reichstag* were content to talk of revolution whilst working for social and political change through the existing system. Such moderation was not generally recognised by the opponents of the Social Democrats. The party was seen as a force for evil, which had to be isolated and controlled. There was no question of it taking part in government.

At the start of the twentieth century, the balance of political forces in the *Reichstag* was important to Germany's political and constitutional problems. The *Reichstag* itself was divided between those who wished to see no change in the existing order and those who wanted the creation of a truly parliamentary democracy in which the imperial government was directly responsible to the *Reichstag* and not to the Kaiser. This may not have presented any problems had the conservative forces been able to maintain a majority. However, the gradual decline in their electoral fortunes, combined with the strength of the Centre Party and the amazing increase in the popularity of the Social Democrats only served to worsen the problem of finding majority support for the passing of legislation. By 1914 this situation showed no sign of being solved since the constitution did not permit measures to be taken to allow for changing circumstances.

Reichstag Election Results, 1887–1912							
Party	1887	1890	1893	1898	1903	1907	1912
German Conservatives	80	73	72	56	54	60	43
Free Conservatives	41	20	28	23	21	24	14
National Liberals	99	42	53	46	51	54	45
Centre	98	106	96	102	100	105	91
Left Liberals	32	76	48	49	36	49	42
Social Democrats	11	35	44	56	81	43	110
Minorites	33	38	35	34	32	29	33
Right-Wing Splinter Parties	3	7	21	31	22	33	19
Total	397	397	397	397	397	397	397

6 Political Forces within Wilhelmine Germany

> **KEY ISSUE** To what extent did the elites manage to maintain their dominant position in Germany?

a) The elites

The problems caused by the political system have led some German historians to move the emphasis of their views about the *Kaiserreich* away from the political centre. The so-called 'structuralist' school appeared in the mid-1960s in the wake of the Fischer controversy. Structuralists sought to explain history through a detailed examination of the various social, political and economic forces that influence events. Foremost amongst the supporters of this approach is H.U. Wehler.

Wehler and his fellow 'structuralists' have rejected the idea that Kaiser Wilhelm II was the main influence behind German policy and political affairs. They have argued that, whereas Bismarck had earlier provided strong leadership, the Kaiser had neither the ability nor the strength of character to do so. In addition they have claimed that, as the powers of both the chancellor and the *Reichstag* were limited by the constitution, after 1890 a power vacuum developed. This led to a situation in which arrogant and overbearing leadership hid the fact that there was always an on-going crisis in German politics.

Wehler has suggested that other forces were able to take advantage of this situation and that these emerged and exerted a major influence over the nation's affairs. By 'other forces' he meant five groups: Prussia's landowning and aristocratic *Junkers*, the officer class of the army, those who held high ranking professional positions in the administration, the judiciary, and senior members of the diplomatic service. Collectively, these five groups are referred to as 'the elites'. He argued that these non-elected elites were able to exercise power because they were Prussians and the constitution had deliberately allowed Prussia to dominate the other German states. Such a situation might possibly have been able to exist if Germany had remained as it had been in 1871 but this was not the case. Germany was undergoing rapid change and new forces were emerging, most notably powerful industrialists, bankers and others engaged in trade and commerce. In addition, class-conscious workers were forming their own movements and becoming more powerful and influential. It was the desire of the elites to maintain their power against what they regarded as a threat to democracy that prompted them to seek an alliance with the newly emerging elites of industry and commerce. They hoped to bring this about by offering them a stake in the system and the promise of armaments contracts and colonial markets overseas. This plan of bringing together the two dominant social elites in order to protect their own status and power has been called *Sammlungspolitik*, a 'policy of concentration'. The strategy was further developed by deliberately disregarding the forces of democracy and socialism and portraying them as unpatriotic enemies of the *Reich*. In the view of Wehler, Germany's decision in the 1890s to undertake *Weltpolitik*, a policy for expanding Germany's influence worldwide, was no more than a form of imperialism or empire building. It was simply an attempt to prop up the position of the elites so that they remained at the top of Germany's class system. The aim was to divert the attention of the masses away from social and political reform and concentrate it instead on winning their support and acceptance of the policies of the Kaiser and the *Kaiserreich*.

Wehler's structuralist views have had enormous influence on our understanding of the *Kaiserreich*, though his views have also attracted much criticism. Does he exaggerate the unity of purpose within the elites? Was imperialism really the main reason for naval construction or was it just a side effect? What is the evidence to support the view that the elites viewed the naval expansion as a step towards achieving a *Sammlungspolitik*? Such basic questions asked of Wehler's views show that his ideas should not be viewed as infallible. Equally, any student of this period must recognise the role of the elites since it is vital to our understanding of Germany's domestic and foreign policies. They must be examined closely as part of our study of Imperial Germany.

Weimar *Reichstag* Election Results, 1919–32								
	1919	1920	1924	1924	1928	1930	1932	1932
Total on register (in millions)	36.8	35.9	38.4	39.0	41.2	43.0	44.2	44.4
Size of poll (per cent)	83.0	79.2	74.4	78.8	75.6	82.0	84.1	80.6
Total no. of seats in *Reichstag*	423	459	472	493	491	577	608	584
NSDAP Seats	–	–	32	14	12	107	230	196
Per Cent	–	–	6.5	3.0	2.6	18.3	37.3	33.1
DNVP Seats	44	71	95	103	73	41	37	52
Per Cent	103	15.1	19.5	20.5	14.2	7.0	5.9	8.3
DVP Seats	19	65	45	51	45	30	7	11
Per Cent	4.4	13.9	9.2	10.1	8.7	4.5	1.2	1.9
ZP/BVP Seats	91	85	81	88	78	87	97	90
Per Cent	19.7	18.0	15.6	17.3	15.2	14.8	15.7	15.0
DDP seats	75	39	28	32	25	20	4	2
Per Cent	18.5	8.3	5.7	6.3	4.9	3.8	1.0	1.0
SPD Seats	165	102	100	131	153	143	133	121
Per Cent	37.9	21.7	20.5	26.0	29.8	24.5	21.6	20.4
USPD Seats	22	84						
Per Cent	7.6	17.9						
KPD Seats	–	4	62	45	54	77	89	100
Per Cent	–	2.1	12.6	9.0	10.8	13.1	14.3	16.9
Other Seats	7	9	29	29	51	72	11	12
Per Cent	1.6	2.9	10.3	7.8	14.0	14.0	2.9	2.9

b) Popular movements

Structuralist theories and the concepts of imperialism and *Sammlungspolitik* that held such sway in the 1970s have now come to be questioned, especially by a new generation of British and American historians. They claim that it offers a theory that at times cannot be convincingly supported by the evidence, or at best can only be supported by carefully selecting the evidence. Others claim that structuralist interpretations concentrate on the elites of German society and ignore other important elements. Some historians have emphasised the need to get away from considering political developments from above and instead to look at 'history from below' in order to recognise the importance of popular movements in the re-shaping of politics at the end of the nineteenth century. In their view the elites lacked any real unity of purpose and therefore they struggled to come to terms with the social upheavals that accompanied the tremendous economic changes in Germany at this time. Their research has not only focused on the labour, *Mittelstand* and agrarian movements, but also on the non-

Prussian regions and the influence of Catholicism. They have tried to shift the historical emphasis away from Prussia and its elites and instead show that the *Kaiserreich* was a state of many regions with very different political and cultural traditions. Many of these interest groups were demanding a genuine voice for the first time, particularly in the wake of the relatively depressed years before 1895. In this way, such historians have successfully highlighted the tremendous growth of political activity in the *Kaiserreich* and also its diversity. This, in turn, has led them to suggest that Germany's political leaders were not so much using but actually responding to public opinion. If this was indeed the case then the policies of Wilhelmine Germany were the result of rather more complicated developments than has previously been thought.

Summary Diagram
The Structure of Wilhelmine Germany

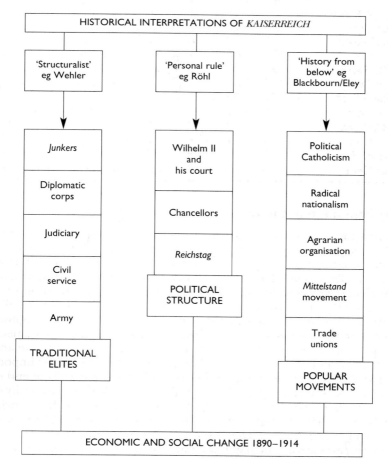

Working on Chapter 2

The aim of this chapter is to help you to gain a 'feel' for the period. It should be seen as complementing very closely Chapter 3, which looks at the actual policies of Wilhelmine Germany. You need to gain an appreciation of the major political, economic and social forces at work in Germany and the beginnings of an understanding of how it has been interpreted by different historians. The chapter is not easy but its understanding will make subsequent chapters easier to follow. Read it again to make absolutely sure that you have understood the important issues raised.

The chapter includes words and phrases that might be new to you. To make sure that you have mastered their understanding complete the following chart:

WORD OR PHRASE	MEANING
Beamte	
bourgeoisie	
Hohenzollern dynasty	
Junker	
Kaiserreich	
Mittelstand	
Sammlungspolitik	
Weltpolitik	

Source-based questions on Chapter 2

GERMAN WORLD POLICY

SOURCE A

1 The entire political situation of Germany is going through a far reaching transformation... many groups are now urging Germany to adopt a world policy... Germany is chiefly a continental power... The desire for a world policy for Germany is in no way in keeping with the strength-
5 ening of Germany's position; it rather puts in question the peaceful intentions of the German Reich...

(From a German newspaper of 1896.)

SOURCE B

1 Political opposition, which was at the time considerable, could only be
   overcome if steady pressure was brought to bear on Parliament by
   public opinion... it was only possible to rouse public opinion by harp-
   ing on nationalism and waking the people to consciousness. The great
5 depression which weighed on the spirit of the people could only be
   lifted if the German Emperor could set before his people a new goal
   towards which to strive, and could indicate to them 'a place in the sun'
   which they must try to attain.

(From the memoirs of von Bulow written in 1914.)

a) What is meant by: i) 'going through a far-reaching transformation'
   (Source A) and ii) 'a place in the sun' (Source B)? (2 × 2 = 4 marks)
b) From your own knowledge, which groups were 'urging Germany to
   adopt a 'world policy'? (4 marks)
c) Compare Sources A and B. To what extent do they agree about the political situation in Germany before the outbreak of the First World War?
   (7 marks)
d) How useful is the source to an understanding of the differing attitudes to
   Weltpolitik in Germany? (To answer the question use your own relevant
   background knowledge as well as the information provided by the
   sources.) (10 marks)

Essay-type questions on Chapter 2

1. To what extent might it be claimed that the rapid economic development of Wilhelmine Germany was responsible for bringing about major
   social and political changes?
2. 'They were the main political force in Imperial Germany.' How valid is
   this assessment of the influence of the elites during the period
   1890–1914?

The Domestic Policies of Imperial Germany, 1890–1914

3

POINTS TO CONSIDER

This chapter contains discussions of the major issues historians have thought are important about domestic politics in Imperial Germany between 1890 and 1914. What you are about to read is therefore an analysis rather than a narrative. 'Facts' are only included when they are needed to illustrate an interpretation which is being described or discussed. As you read this chapter for the first time make notes summarising as briefly as you can the 'flow of ideas' of the chapter. Try to read several paragraphs between each pause for note making.

KEY DATES

1890	Resignation of Bismarck. Caprivi appointed Chancellor
1891	Bilateral commercial treaties with other European countries
1893	Agrarian League formed
1894	Hohenlohe-Schillingsfurst appointed Chancellor
1897	First Naval Bill passed
1898	Naval League formed
1900	Second Naval Bill passed
1908	The *Daily Telegraph* affair
1912	Major socialist gains in elections to *Reichstag*
	Third Naval Bill passed
1913	Zabern incident
1914	Outbreak of the First World War

1 Domestic Affairs, 1890–1914

KEY ISSUE Why was the issue of tariffs so important to German economic policy?

a) Caprivi's 'new course'

If Wilhelm II had assumed that Bismarck's departure would give him a free hand, he was to be disappointed. The new chancellor, Count Leo von Caprivi, proved to be more astute and independent-minded than the Kaiser had bargained for. Caprivi soon embarked on what he referred to as a 'new course', which involved a more consultative approach to government and a conciliatory attitude to previously hostile forces, such as the Centre Party and the Social Democrats. In contrast to the stalemate between Bismarck and the *Reichstag* in the late 1880s, Caprivi was able to depend on a fair degree of backing from the *Reichstag*. This allowed him to push through a number of social measures in 1891 which included the prohibition of Sunday work and limitations on child and female labour. Such success paved the way for an even more important change – the reform of Germany's policy of imposing taxes, called tariffs, on goods imported into the country. Ever since 1879 Germany had followed a policy of protection for both agriculture and industry. However, this led to a shortage of wheat and a marked rise in food prices. In order to encourage the export of German manufactured goods, between 1891 and 1894 Caprivi negotiated a series of commercial treaties with Austria-Hungary, Italy, Russia and a number of smaller states. These treaties were bilateral which meant that each country agreed changes likely to benefit the other. These agreements led to the reduction in German tariffs on agricultural goods in return for favourable reductions in the tariffs imposed on exported German manufactured goods. Therefore, they not only acted as a vital spur to the growth of the German economy, but they also represented a political triumph for Caprivi. His policy of tariff reform gained broad support, as most parties, except the Conservatives, recognised the benefits of lower food prices. It seemed as if the new chancellor could perhaps make Bismarck's system work in a flexible and progressive fashion. It was not to last.

b) Caprivi – growing opposition and resignation

To start with Wilhelm II stood by Caprivi's policy in the belief that the improvements would discourage people from supporting the socialists. Indeed, the Kaiser had been so taken by the success of tariff reform that Caprivi had been given the noble title of count. However, many of Wilhelm's advisers at court had been upset by Caprivi's socialist policies and they increasingly encouraged the Kaiser to ditch him and to assume a more authoritarian 'personal rule'. The landowning interest, in particular, which was so well represented in courtly circles, was deeply upset by the commercial treaties since they threatened to reduce their profits. In 1893 the Agrarian League (*Bund der Landwirte*) was formed to put pressure on parliament and to win support and privileges for landowners. It quickly grew into an effective and well-organised lobby of a quarter of a million members that acted as a powerful pressure group on behalf of the Conservatives. In addition, during 1892–3 there had also been resentment in military circles when Caprivi had made concessions to the *Reichstag* by reducing an Army Bill that reduced national service (the length of time all young men had to serve in the army) from three years to two. Conservative opposition to Caprivi's 'new course' reinforced

Wilhelm II's own doubts about his chancellor's suitability for office. In 1894 events came to a head when, frightened by a series of anarchist outrages throughout Europe and worried by the success in the previous year of the Social Democrats who increased their total number of seats to 44, Wilhelm II pressed Caprivi to draw up an anti-socialist Subversion Bill. The chancellor refused and this led to an extraordinary plan by Wilhelm II and his supporter, Count Eulenburg, to set aside the powers of the *Reichstag*, crush socialism and establish a more authoritarian system centred on the Kaiser himself. This was the final straw for Caprivi. He successfully talked the Kaiser out of such a course of action, but he had lost the will to carry on. In October 1894 Caprivi resigned and gladly retired from the political scene. His four years as chancellor neatly illustrate the difficulties of trying to cope with the pressures of the various political forces in Imperial Germany. In his attempt to create a genuine base of parliamentary support for the government, Caprivi showed his understanding of the need, in a modern industrial society, for a political approach that recognised the concerns and aspirations of the mass of the population. However, Caprivi's 'new course' foundered because it attracted the opposition of the established forces of power and influence. He was subjected to considerable abuse from the conservative press and he was the focus of opposition intrigue at court. In the end, he could not rely on the consistent support of the Kaiser whose delusions of greatness was now taken up with thoughts of 'personal rule' and Weltpolitik.

2 *Weltpolitik* and Domestic Policy

> **KEY ISSUE** What were the aims of *Weltpolitik*?

a) *Weltpolitik*

In 1894, the seventy-five year old Prince Hohenlohe-Schillingsfurst was appointed Chancellor. During the next six years, men who supported the policies of the Kaiser increasingly dominated the government. The ageing Hohenlohe-Schillingsfurst was no match for the intrigue at court and in government circles and by 1897 a group of key political figures had emerged which sympathised with the Kaiser's wish to embark on what he saw as personal rule. In that year there were three new appointments to important positions in the government – Admiral von Tirpitz, as navy secretary; Count Posadowsky-Wehner, as interior minister; and most importantly von Bülow, as foreign minister. In addition, two long serving figures began to assume even greater prominence. These were Friedrich von Holstein, a senior official in the Foreign Office; and Johannes von Miquel, Prussian Finance Minister (and leader of the National Liberals). The emergence of this government team has led many historians to view 1897 as an important turning-point in German history because it was also the year in which the drive to achieve world power status for Germany, or *Weltpolitik*, was started. This policy involved increasing the size of Germany's colonial empire, the creation of economic spheres of influence and the expansion of German naval power to complement the strength of the army. This not only marked a decisive shift in the emphasis of Germany's foreign policy, but also had all sorts of implications for the future of German domestic politics.

b) Why did *Weltpolitik* become government policy?

Certainly, the Kaiser himself believed in Germany's destiny to become a world power, and in the government team assembled in 1897 he had a number of like-minded ministers. However, there were also other powerful forces at work in Germany that favoured the new policy. Industrialisation had created economic demands for the acquisition of raw materials and markets beyond Europe. So, at a time when European powers were expanding their overseas empires, any push to extend the German economic sphere of influence needed political backing. German nationalism was also being seen in a different light. The nationalistic spirit encouraged by German unification was giving way to the ideas of Social Darwinism – natural selection through the survival of the fittest and the unending struggle for supremacy between nations. Some believed that the survival of Germany as a leading nation required a more active part in world affairs. Finally, economic changes and new thinking also contributed to the emergence of new political forces. The 1890s not only witnessed the rise of the Social Democrats, but also a series of populist right-wing movements, that reflected the changing attitudes of the peasantry and the *Mittelstand* (see page 14). These nationalists formed a series of pressure groups of which the most infamous was the Pan-German League, the *Alldeutscher Verband*. Such groups were anti-socialist, racist, anti-Semitic, expansionist and inevitably strong supporters of any policy that advanced German power and influence. They therefore performed a two-fold purpose. On the one hand, they popularised the idea of *Weltpolitik* and encouraged mass support for the policy. On the other, they exerted political pressure on the imperial government to pursue the policy to the full.

c) Support for *Weltpolitik*

Of great importance to *Weltpolitik* was the decision to expand the German navy. The appointment of Tirpitz meant that there was a man prepared to do this, for he not only enjoyed the full confidence of Wilhelm II, but he also recognised the importance of gaining parliamentary support and popular backing for the plans. With these aims in mind, he established the Navy League (*Flottenverein*) in 1898. The Navy League argued that naval expansion was a patriotic national symbol of Germany's new status in the world. With the backing of leading industrialists, it was able to gain a membership of over one million and this large scale public support strengthened Tirpitz's position in his handling of the *Reichstag*. When he presented the Naval Bills of 1898 and 1900 they were both passed with substantial majorities, largely because they were supported by the Centre Party.

The introduction of Weltpolitik succeeded where Caprivi's 'new course' had run into difficulties because it achieved a greater acceptance from the various political parties. It successfully rallied both the middle and upper classes and their political representatives in the *Reichstag* behind the Kaiser and the government. The support of the Centre Party represented an important step forward, since it helped secure an effective majority for the government in the *Reichstag*. *Weltpolitik* even won the support of many of the ordinary people by playing on their feelings of patriotism and loyalty to the crown. Finally, it was a policy that closely coincided with the aspirations of the Kaiser who convinced himself that domestic policy must therefore at last be under his personal rule. In 1900, Hohenlohe-Schillingsfurst, tired of being ignored and not consulted on policy matter, resigned.

d) Bülow and the problems of *Weltpolitik*

However, *Weltpolitik* did not prove to be the complete cure for the problems of government. Far from it, Bülow, who was made chancellor in 1900, found that in spite of his close relationship with the Kaiser, the government was still subject to ever increasing pressures. It was not always so easy to maintain a government majority, as was shown most obviously by the political struggle over the renewal of Caprivi's commercial treaties. From the start, the Conservatives working with the Agrarian League had bitterly opposed the agreements, whilst the Left Liberals and the Social Democrats remained committed to lower tariffs. In the end the compromise Tariff Law of 1902 restored tariffs to 1892 levels, which was well short of the Conservatives' demands, and it was only carried by a combination of the Centre, the National Liberals and Free Conservatives. *Weltpolitik* generated its own problems too. The budget had run into debt as the mounting costs of maintaining the army, expanding the navy and running the empire took effect. If *Weltpolitik* were to be continued then substantial tax increases had to be introduced. Bülow was astute enough to realise that this was likely to cause a political storm and so it did. In 1905 he suggested a two-pronged attack on the deficit by proposing an increase in indirect taxes and an inheritance tax. The proposals came to nothing because the Centre and the Social Democrats voted down the indirect taxes that would have hit the working classes most severely. In addition, the Conservatives and their allies weakened the inheritance tax so as to make it financially insignificant. As a result, the debt continued to grow. Meanwhile Bülow's government was also being attacked for its policy in the colony of South West Africa where, in 1904–5, a native revolt had been crushed. Subsequent revelations of brutality and incompetence in the administration of the colony encouraged the Centre Party and others to vote against the government's proposal to provide extra money for the colonial administration.

During the early years of the twentieth century, the German political system became increasingly sophisticated. New political forces were at work in the country and yet government, which was traditionally in the hands of conservatives, showed only a limited capacity to come to terms with these forces. Powerful interest groups, such as the trade unions and the Catholic Church, were no longer prepared to be ignored and they expected their political representatives to make their voices felt in parliament. Economic forces also exerted new pressures. The problems of the budget and tariff reform reveal clearly the limitations on implementing government policy and how this, in turn, created further political pressures. By 1906 it seemed as if Bülow's government, far from controlling events, was increasingly at the mercy of them.

3 The *Daily Telegraph* Affair

> **KEY ISSUE** Why did the *Daily Telegraph* Affair lead to a crisis in the relationship between the Kaiser and his Chancellor, Bulow?

Despite these defeats, Bülow retained the support of the Kaiser and in 1907 the government gained a good result in the so-called 'Hottentot' election, named after the rebels in South West Africa. The government's election campaign was openly nationalistic, anti-socialist and anti-Catholic. This enabled Bülow to bring together the Conservatives, Free Conservatives, National Liberals and Left Liberals in a coalition dubbed the 'Bülow bloc'. However, Bülow's triumph could not and did not last long. His coalition was extremely fragile. The difference between what the government received from taxation and spent, the budgetary deficit, was an increasingly serious problem. In the winter of 1908–9 the political crisis came to a head, although in a somewhat bizarre fashion. The German public had already been treated to a moral scandal by the revelation that the Kaiser's close friend, Eulenburg, was at the centre of an extensive ring of homosexuals at court, when the *Daily Telegraph* Affair broke (see account below).

a) The reported interview

The Kaiser's *Daily Telegraph* interview with Colonel Stuart Wortley:

1   As I have said His Majesty honoured me with a long conversation and
spoke with impulsive and unusual frankness. 'You English' he said 'are
mad, mad as March Hares. What has come over you that you are so
completely given over to suspicions quite unworthy of a great nation?
5   What more can I do than I have done? I declared with all the emphasis
at my command in my speech at the Guildhall that my heart is set upon
peace, and that it is one of my dearest wishes to live on the best of
terms with England. Have I ever been false to my word? Falsehood and
prevarication are alien to my nature. My actions ought to speak for
10 themselves, but you listen not to them but to those who misinterpret
them. That is a personal insult which I feel and resent. . .'
    'I repeat' continued His Majesty 'that I am a friend of England but you
make it hard for me to remain so. *My task is not the easiest. The prevailing sentiment amongst my own people is not friendly to England. I am in a*
15 *minority in my own land but it is a minority of the best elements. . .* *
    But you will say, what of the German Navy? Is not that a menace
to England? Against whom but England is it being steadily built up? If
England is not in the minds of those Germans who are bent on creating a powerful fleet, why is Germany asked to consent to such new
20 and heavy burdens of taxation? My answer is clear. Germany is a
young and growing Empire. She has a world-wide commerce which is
rapidly expanding, and to which the legitimate ambition of patriotic
Germans refuses to assign any bounds. Germany must have a powerful fleet to protect that commerce and her manifold interests in even
25 the most distant seas. She expects those interests to go on growing
and she must be able to champion them manfully in any quarter of the
globe. . . Only those powers which have vast navies will be listened to
with respect when the future of the Pacific areas comes to be solved,
and for that reason only Germany must have a powerful fleet. It may
30 even be that England herself will be glad that Germany has a fleet,
when they speak together on the same side in the great debates of the
future. . .'

*For the words in italics the German Foreign Ministry recommended
instead: 'The prevailing sentiment amongst large parts of the middle
and lower classes of my own people is not friendly to England. So I am
so to say in a minority.'

Wilhelm II's comments attracted much criticism and there were
demands in the *Reichstag* for constitutional restraints to be placed on
the Kaiser. However, Bülow himself was in a difficult position, since
he had actually cleared the article before publication. The delicacy of
the constitutional situation is revealed in a letter written in November
1908 by the British ambassador to his foreign secretary:

1 Prince Bülow spoke at some length and in a very depressed tone of the present crisis in Germany. He said that the Emperor meant so well, but the fact was that, as Bismarck had said, there is no longer room for absolutism in Germany. Parliamentary government was with their
5 countless parties, impossible, but what people clamoured for, and meant to have, was constitutional government. Germany was intensely monarchical and this crisis with its unusually hot outcry against the Sovereign, would, he hoped, pass as other similar crises had passed: but nevertheless, the present feeling against the personal influence of the
10 Emperor in public affairs was very strong, stronger than it had ever been before, and it caused him considerable anxiety. There must in fact be a change; he spoke feelingly on the subject, because, as I had perhaps noticed, his position as things were now, was anything but comfortable.

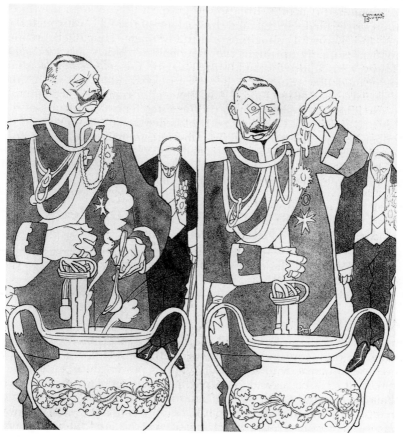

Divination by Molten Lead
'We'll just see what the future brings forth.'
'Confound it, that looks like a muzzle.'

b) The outcome

Caught between loyalty to his friend, the Kaiser, and the demands of the *Reichstag*, Bülow sided with the latter. He secured a promise from the Kaiser that, in future, the terms of the constitution would be respected. Thereafter, the crisis petered out and no constitutional changes followed. It seemed as if Bülow, nicknamed 'the eel', had once again slithered his way out of a tight corner, but the Kaiser's trust in his Chancellor had been fatally weakened by these events and when Bülow's budget proposals were rejected in 1909 the Kaiser secured the Chancellor's resignation.

The *Daily Telegraph* Affair provides an illuminating insight into the power politics of the Wilhelmine age. Bülow had survived for over a decade at the very centre of German politics by playing the part of the old-fashioned courtier with a sound grasp of how to keep the vested interests satisfied. He retained the backing of the Kaiser through flattery and by turning situations to his advantage. He gained broader political support through the nationalistic policy of *Weltpolitik*. However, his failure to stand by the Kaiser in the *Daily Telegraph* Affair underlined how vulnerable the office of chancellor still was to the personal whims of the Kaiser. The Chancellor remained accountable to the Kaiser alone and not to the *Reichstag*. This was in spite of the fact that there was a growing body of belief that the Kaiser could no longer behave as an all powerful, absolute monarch, but must conform to certain constitutional formalities. Yet now when the opportunity presented itself for constitutional reform, the *Reichstag* showed a marked reluctance to assert itself and its authority.

4 Political Developments During the Years Before the Outbreak of War

> **KEY ISSUE** Why did the German government reach a position of political stalemate?

a) Stalemate

In the last few years of peace, the German government was nominally in the hands of Chancellor Bethmann-Hollweg. However, because his capacity to rule was limited by powerful forces, between 1909 and 1914 he backed away from introducing major initiatives. It seemed as if the German government had reached political stalemate. Bethmann-Hollweg's parliamentary base of support was narrow. His conservative views meant that his natural allies came from the right-wing parties. Any attempt to broaden his support by appealing to the centre or left would have offended his conservative and right-wing supporters. In this situation Bethmann-Hollweg tried to avoid depending on any particular group of parties. This led him to become increasingly influenced by groups outside parliament, particularly the army. As a result, the military assumed an increasingly influential role. The British historian Gordon Craig maintains that 'the militarisation of Wilhelminian society reached its height during the peace-time years of Bethmann-Hollweg's chancellorship'. The *Reichstag* elections of 1912 further added to the Chancellor's parliamentary difficulties, since there was a distinct shift to the left with the Social Democrats and a united group of Left Liberals winning 110 and 42 seats respectively. This created a situation of virtual deadlock for the German government. It also served to increase the fears of conservatives of a possible democratic and socialist revolution.

5 The Crises of 1912–13

> **KEY ISSUE** Were the measures taken by the government to deal with the crises of 1912–13 successful?

a) The demand for increased military spending

However, in the long term there was no way to avoid the approaching crisis caused by the country's economic problems and the conflicting demands of imperial finance and defence expenditure came to a head. In the wake of the Second Moroccan Crisis (see page 52) the army and the navy both submitted plans involving major increases in expenditure plans. The idea of an inheritance tax was again proposed as the only possible means of raising the required money, but Bethmann-Hollweg feared a hostile political reaction and resorted to the stop-gap measure of taxing spirits. In early 1913 Moltke, the Chief of Staff, went even further and demanded a second Army Bill to increase the peace-time strength of the army by 20 per cent to 800,000 men in 1914. Such massive increases could only be met by a significant change in the attitude of the *Reichstag*. Fortunately for Bethmann-Hollweg the inheritance tax was accepted. The worsening international situation undoubtedly acted as a significant stimulus. The confused state of German politics was revealed by the fact that the Conservatives, who supported the increased military expenditure, opposed it, whilst the Social Democrats, who were traditionally against military spending, supported it! For the socialists, the attraction was that the tax established a precedent of a property-based tax.

b) The Zabern affair

Just before the outbreak of war German domestic politics was rocked by one further crisis, the Zabern affair, which clearly highlighted the divisions in German politics and society. After a series of disturbances in the Alsatian town of Zabern in 1913, army officers overruled the civilian authorities and arrested a number of local people. In one incident, an officer used his sabre to cut down a lame cobbler. Criticism of the army officers was based on the way they had ignored citizens' rights and placed the army above the law. The army defended itself by claiming to be accountable to the Kaiser alone – and Wilhelm condoned the action. In the *Reichstag*, Bethmann-Hollweg, unlike Bülow in 1908, stood by the army and the Kaiser, but the political opposition was intense and the Chancellor received a massive vote of no-confidence. For historians such as Röhl, the Zabern affair shows how, right up to 1914, the Kaiserreich was still dominated by the actions, decisions and personality of the Kaiser and his entourage. The very fact that Bethmann-Hollweg was able to continue as Chancellor despite a major defeat in the *Reichstag* is seen as proof enough of how the Kaiser still ultimately controlled policy and political decision-making. For the structuralists, Wilhelm II was never more than a 'shadow Kaiser'. He was considered a front for the elites who were determined to manipulate him, the system and government policy in order to preserve their own privileged positions. In this interpretation, the Zabern affair is seen as a classic example of how the army was able to preserve its own authority and status despite the huge public outcry at its action. The Zabern affair is also clear evidence of how popular pressures were bubbling up in order to bring about genuine democratic and social change.

c) Conclusion

The real danger when trying to draw conclusions about the government of Imperial Germany is that one can be easily drawn into making over-simple generalisations about a period of history which lasted nearly a quarter of a century when, in fact, any convincing explanation needs to contain carefully balanced points. Between 1890 and 1914, the political situation was always fluid and in reaching any conclusion it is necessary to recognise how the balance between the various political forces was continually changing. This is a most demanding task for almost all students, and is likely to be very frustrating for those who crave certainty. Perhaps it would be best to recognise that an analysis of the *Kaiserreich* will probably require conclusions of a tentative nature. What follows is merely one possible interpretation. It should not be viewed as final, or as in any sense the 'right' answer. It is presented in the hope that it will form a basis for further discussion.

It is impossible to cast aside the Kaiser entirely. In a way, it has been suggested, Wilhelm II came to symbolise the inconsistencies of the *Kaiserreich*. On the one hand, he was a defender of traditional privileges of the Prussian monarchy. On the other, he was an enthusiast for technology, new industries and a world role for Germany. From 1890 to 1914, his personal influence enabled him to decide the framework of government policy. Between 1897 and 1908 his influence was most marked. This represented the high-point of the Kaiser's personal rule and it coincided exactly with the years of supremacy of Bülow who recognised that his own position depended on flattery and the promotion of the Kaiser's personal views. However, the Kaiser was not an absolute monarch since the constitutional framework limited his political power. There also existed powerful forces that acted to both influence and limit his power. For example, the Prussian elites greatly influenced the working of Wilhelmine Germany. Bülow recognised their political significance and developed policies that did much to protect their interests. Caprivi, on the other hand, had paid the price of alienating them in the early 1890s. Later on, after the Eulenburg and *Daily Telegraph* scandals, when Wilhelm II's personal position was weakened and the international situation grew more tense, the military clique gained an increasingly influential role at court and in government. However, even then one must guard against presenting a too generalised picture that portrays the elites as manipulating and dominating the whole political system. There were other forces at work that reflected Germany's earlier history and the more recent economic and social developments that transformed the country into a modern state. Between 1890 and 1914 these forces became an increasingly important factor in the political struggles of the time. Consequently, although in 1914 the balance of power still rested with the forces of conservatism, it is also clear that their right to govern was under threat and their ability to govern as they would have liked was already being limited by the forces of change. The conflict between these two sets of forces was the source of great political tension. By 1914 Imperial Germany was not yet ungovernable, partly because its economic well-being limited the spread of discontent and also because there was still general respect for the monarchy. However, it had reached a situation of political stalemate that made for weak and confused government. The *Kaiserreich* was both socially and politically very complicated. It was just as complex as the Kaiser's own eccentric personality. As the historian P. Kennedy has written: 'the Kaiser both reflected and inter-meshed (was involved in) the country's broader problems'.

Summary Diagram
The Policies of Wilhelmine Germany

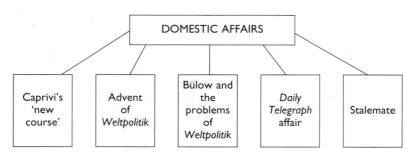

Working on Chapter 3

This chapter has taken a broad look at the political developments in Germany during the years 1890–1914. It is intended to provide you with an understanding of the period that will allow you to make your own judgements and attempt your own analysis of the problems that beset the country's domestic affairs.

A good way to take yourself through the process of making your own judgements about what you have read would be to attempt brief answers to the following four questions:

1. Where did the political power in Germany really lie?
2. What was the relationship between the Kaiser and the *Reichstag*?
3. To what extent did political tensions at home influence the decision to embark on a policy of *Weltpolitik*?
4. What were the significance and impact of the crises brought about by the *Daily Telegraph* and Zabern affairs?

Finally, you could attempt to pull all your ideas on this chapter together by summing up the state of German politics in 1914.

Answering structured and interpretation questions on Chapter 3

Structured questions are structured in the sense that they are sub-divided into parts. It is usual that each successive part requires a more detailed and lengthier answer. You will see that the allocation of marks for each part reflects these differences. You will be expected to present historical explanations and show your understanding of historical concepts. You must also communicate your knowledge and understanding in a clear and relevant manner. You could help further develop your skills by answering whichever of the following questions fits the style of examination paper you will be sitting.

1. a) In international trade what is meant by a protectionism? (*2 marks*)
   b) What benefits does a bilateral trade agreement bring to the countries involved? (*3 marks*)
   c) Explain briefly why German landowners were opposed to Caprivi's tariff reforms. (*5 marks*)
   d) In following his 'new course' did Caprivi show that he was aware of the needs of a modern industrial society? Explain your answer fully. (*10 marks*)

2. a) What is meant by the term *Weltpolitik*? (*2 marks*)
   b) Explain briefly why the Kaiser considered the expansion of the German navy to be essential. (*3 marks*)
   c) Why did the *Daily Telegraph* affair prove to be an embarrassment to Wilhelm II? (*5 marks*)
   d) Had Wilhelm II managed to establish his personal rule in Germany by 1914? Explain your answer fully. (*10 marks*)

Essay-type questions on Chapter 3

'A period during which the policies of Imperial Germany were mainly decided by pressure groups.' (K. Perry, a modern British historian, in *Modern European History*, 1976.) How valid is this interpretation of German politics during the period 1890 to 1914? (*25 marks*)

German Foreign Policy, 1890–1914. The Origins of the First World War

POINTS TO CONSIDER

The part played by Germany in the events leading to the First World War and the extent of her responsibility for that war are the main issues considered in this chapter. Note how German foreign policy changed after the resignation of Bismarck in 1890. Consider too the ambitions of Kaiser Wilhelm II made evident in his decision to follow a policy of *Weltpolitik* (see also Chapter 3). You will also need to note the ways in which German foreign policy affected her relations with other major powers – particularly Britain and France – and influenced developments in Europe generally.

KEY DATES

1905	Schlieffen Plan devised
1893	Pan German League formed
1896	Kruger Telegram sent
1897	Bülow's 'place in the sun' speech
1905	Tangier incident
1907	Britain, France and Russia form Triple *Entente*
1908	Bosnian crisis
1911	Agadir crisis
1912	Anglo-German Naval Conference and First Balkan War
1913	Second Balkan War
1914	Start of First World War

1 Germany and the European Situation

> **KEY ISSUE** After 1890, to what extent did German foreign policy become aggressive?

a) German foreign policy

Why has the foreign policy of Imperial Germany been such an important area of historical debate over the years? Initially it was because, when the Treaty of Versailles which ended the First World War was negotiated in 1919, the Allies insisted on Germany accepting responsibility for the war by signing a War Guilt Clause. This led to an extensive debate in the inter-war years, which eventually resulted in a general agreement that the European Great Powers had stumbled into war because of the system of alliances and the state of international relations. It was decided that no one country could be blamed for causing the war. It was a view that proved acceptable to many German historians. It was not until the early 1960s that the then generally accepted view about the causes of the First World War was challenged. The publication in 1961 of Fritz Fischer's *Griff nach der Weltmacht* (Germany's Aims in the First World War) put forward the idea that the German government did bear the decisive share of responsibility for starting the war in 1914. Fischer argued this on the basis of what he saw as its unquestionable desire to achieve German predominance throughout Europe. Fischer's interpretation caused enormous controversy among German historians. This led to protracted squabbling and even to offensive name-calling. However, Fischer himself was not moved from his point of view and in 1969 he published another book *Krieg der Illusionen* (War of Illusions). In this he suggested that from the time of the Second Moroccan Crisis in 1911 (see page 52) the German leadership consistently pursued a policy aimed at fighting a European war as a means of achieving world-power status for Germany. Fischer's views led to a historical controversy the reverberations of which continue to this day. Although the bad feeling is now less, there remain basic differences of opinion about the motives and direction of German foreign policy during the pre-war years. There are five key questions that need to be answered in this chapter. Firstly, did the break-up of the Bismarck system of alliances after 1890 set in motion a chain of disasters that led towards the catastrophe of the outbreak of the First World War? Secondly, at the start of the century did the coming of *Weltpolitik* pose a real threat to the existing European situation? Thirdly, why did attempts to bring about some improvement in Anglo-German relations fail? Fourthly, how convincing is the evidence that Germany was planning a war in the years before 1914? Finally, how far was Germany responsible for the turn of events in the summer of 1914?

b) The end of the Bismarckian System, 1890–7

After 1871, Bismarck used diplomacy to ensure the isolation of Germany's major continental enemy, France. He achieved this by establishing a close relationship with the two neighbouring empires (Austria-Hungary and Russia), to which was added Italy in 1882. He worked hard to retain the friendship of both Austria-Hungary and Russia, but in the end had to show a preference for one or the other. He chose Austria-Hungary, with the result that Russia felt somewhat slighted despite the fact that Bismarck signed a separate three-year Reinsurance Treaty with her in 1887. He also made a conscious effort not to antagonise Britain.

In the seven years after Bismarck's fall Germany's international position changed dramatically. There were those who believed that the Reinsurance Treaty conflicted with Germany's other commitments, especially to Austria-Hungary. In March 1890 it was allowed to lapse. Such an understanding of the Reinsurance Treaty may well have been correct, but the result was to push Russia into the arms of France. In 1892 the two powers signed a military agreement that formed the basis of the Franco-Russian Alliance of 1894–5. This alliance made a reality of what Bismarck called a 'nightmare of coalitions' since it meant that at some time in the future Germany might have to fight a war on two fronts – against France in the west and Russia in the east.

c) Anglo-German relations

Reaching some kind of understanding with Britain might have lessened such a danger since it would have lessened the chances of an Anglo-French alliance and strengthened the German position. Unfortunately diplomatic moves in 1894 failed to bring this about and consequently attempts to provide a firm basis for a mutual understanding came to nothing. Indeed, only two years later Anglo-German relations went sharply into reverse over the 'Kruger Telegram'. In 1896, relations between the British and former Dutch (Boer) settlers in South Africa reached crisis point following an attempted invasion of a Boer province, the Transvaal. The British were offended when the German Kaiser sent a congratulatory note to the President of the Transvaal, Paul Kruger, for resisting British interference in his country. It led the Boers to believe that they could expect German support in any future conflict with the British.

It is tempting to conclude that, by 1897, Germany's international standing was in decline. It could, for example, be argued that control of foreign policy had passed into the hands of lesser politicians who had allowed Bismarck's system to collapse, and that Germany was already firmly on a path that was to lead to war in 1914. However, such a view is heavily influenced by our knowledge of how events were to unfold in later years. It is true that, when compared with the years before, Germany's foreign policy after 1890 seems to be lacking in direction, but it must be remembered that Bismarck's system of alliances was not itself without fault and that cracks had already begun to appear in the system. Relations between Germany and Russia had already deteriorated before Bismarck's dismissal and there were those who saw the Reinsurance Treaty as no more than a temporary measure. Moreover, since 1890, Germany had deliberately pursued what has been referred to as a 'free-hand' policy. It was hoped that disagreements might occur amongst the other European powers and that this, combined with more friendly German approaches, would lead to Germany having a major voice in European affairs. By 1897 Germany had allies in Austria-Hungary and Italy as well as an improved relationship with France. Relations with Russia were also slowly recovering. Even though the Kruger Telegram had upset Britain, the fact was that Britain was on far worse terms with Russia and France, than she was with Germany. German foreign policy had moved on from the days of Bismarck and, although the Franco-Russian alliance was still regarded as a threat, the situation was not regarded as immediately dangerous.

2 The Coming of *Weltpolitik*, 1897–1907

> **KEY ISSUE** To what extent did the decision to follow a policy of *Weltpolitik* affect German foreign policy?

The decision to pursue *Weltpolitik* in 1897 was an important moment in German history. In Chapter 3, we saw how this coincided with important changes on the political scene at home. It was also an important turning point in the development of German foreign policy. *Weltpolitik* meant different things to different people. For some, it meant the chance to create a larger overseas empire by the acquisition of colonies and so aid further the expansion of the German economy. For others, it was simply a policy to assist German business to establish areas of economic influence in as many parts of the world as possible. Another view, made evident by the Pan-German League, a movement that came into being in 1893 to encourage the union of all German-speaking peoples, amounted to nothing less than racist *Lebensraum*. *Lebensraum* was a policy that favoured territorial expansion in order to create more living space for the German people. It encouraged colonial expansion and the conquest of neighbouring countries particularly those along Germany's eastern frontiers.

a) Views of *Weltpolitik*

At the time, these differences of opinion were reflected at the highest levels of the German establishment. The structuralists regard *Weltpolitik* as no more than a change in domestic politics (see page 35). Others maintain that in 1897 Germany embarked on a course aimed at achieving equality with the British Empire and possibly even more. This push for world supremacy was to be achieved by policies that included the expansion of the navy, the creation of a large colonial empire in Africa, and the economic domination of Europe by Germany's interests. In Fischer's view, *Weltpolitik* was a grand plan involving both continental and overseas expansion in order to attain world-power status.

Attractive as Fischer's interpretation may seem, it gives the impression that, after 1897, the direction of German foreign policy followed an orderly pattern. If Fischer's understanding of *Weltpolitik* is accurate, why then was German policy so confusing? Between 1897 and 1907 the real achievements of *Weltpolitik* were very limited. Certainly, naval construction was started and German economic influence was extended into South America, China, the Near East and the Balkans. However, Germany's small and costly empire only gained the Chinese port of Kiaochow (1897) and a few islands in the Pacific (1899). Moreover, some of the consequences of *Weltpolitik* proved disastrous. Some believed that the policy of maintaining a free hand was consistent with *Weltpolitik* and they believed that Britain and Russia would remain at loggerheads. Consequently, between 1898 and 1901 Germany showed little enthusiasm for British requests for an alliance. Instead, as a result of anti-British feeling brought about by the Boer War and the British view that the German navy posed a threat, relations between the two countries worsened. What had not been considered was the possibility that Britain would reduce her fears of isolation by signing an alliance with Japan (1902) and the *Entente Cordiale*, with France (1904). Whilst the former was limited to the Pacific area, the latter, despite the fact that it was an agreement to settle differences rather than a formal alliance, was likely to encourage future diplomatic co-operation between the two countries. However, there was no disguising the fact that Britain had been offended and that Germany could no longer rely on Anglo-French hostility to strengthen its own hand. It was the desire to break the *Entente* that prompted Germany to provoke the Moroccan Crisis of 1905–6. By claiming to support Moroccan independence in a territory that had become an accepted French sphere of influence, Bülow hoped to reveal the flimsy nature of Britain's loyalty to the *Entente*. It was not to be. At the international conference held at Algeçiras in 1906, Germany suffered a major diplomatic humiliation. She found herself diplomatically isolated and France got its way over Morocco. The *entente* had stood firm. In fact, as a result of Germany's pressure, it had been strengthened. To make matters worse, a year later Britain signed an *entente* with Russia (1907).

The decision to embark on *Weltpolitik* in 1897 was probably, at first, no more than a desire felt in Germany that it was time for the country to catch up with the other major European powers. This meant different things to different people. The thinking of the leading figures differed and so there was much confusion. There was no real planning and consequently, after ten years of *Weltpolitik,* Germany found herself in a state of diplomatic confusion. The real benefits of *Weltpolitik* remained limited to the commercial advantages from overseas economic expansion and the prestige arising from possessing a powerful army and navy. However, Germany's colonial possessions remained few. In this sense, at very considerable financial cost, *Weltpolitik* had made very little progress towards promoting Germany to world-power status. It could therefore be argued, as many Germans did at the time, that the policy did not pose a threat to anyone else.

However, *Weltpolitik* was not seen this way outside Germany. Britain had been alienated and had taken steps to maintain a significant naval lead. At the same time, she had aligned herself with France and Russia in the Triple *Entente*. As a result, Germany's diplomatic and strategic position was weaker in 1907 than it had been for a generation or so before. In this sense *Weltpolitik* contributed to an important change in the European situation.

3 The Road to War

> **KEY ISSUE** Why did attempts to improve Anglo-German relations fail?

a) Attempts to improve Anglo-German relations (1907–11)

By 1907 the major powers of Europe were already divided along lines that would parallel those of 1914. It might be thought that there was now no turning back. However, such a view can not be held with certainty. A series of crises in Bosnia (1908–9), and Morocco (1911), as well as the Balkan Wars (1912–13) passed off without the outbreak of major European war. It should also be remembered that genuine efforts were made during that time to improve the relationship between Britain and Germany. If an Anglo-German *entente* had been agreed, then the situation that arose in 1914 would have been very different indeed! In 1909, Anglo-German relations reached a decidedly low point. During that year Austria-Hungary annexed her small Balkan neighbour Bosnia. Bosnia's neighbour Serbia, as well as members of the Triple *Entente*, resented the action. When Germany supported the Austrian annexation, doubts arose within the Triple *Entente* about the true purpose of German foreign policy. This was especially true in Britain, since it coincided with a renewed concern over the worrying issue of increasing German naval strength. Despite the financial problems faced by the German government (see page 42), Bülow had accepted Tirpitz's proposal of two supplementary naval laws in 1906 and 1908 which were intended to bring about a considerable growth in the German navy. Britain was seriously concerned that her naval supremacy was threatened and that the increase in the size of German navy was intended to challenge it. The reaction in Britain came to a head in 1909 when the British government decided to increase naval expenditure substantially in order to maintain her lead. Consequently, Britain and Germany became involved in an expensive naval arms race that worsened an already uneasy relationship.

The appointment of Bethmann-Hollweg as German Chancellor was followed by an attempt to improve Anglo-German relations. He recognised that an agreement with Britain to limit naval construction would not only reduce his country's financial difficulties, but could also loosen Britain's ties to the Triple *Entente*. There were also influential people in Britain who saw the advantages of a settlement of Anglo-German differences. During negotiations carried on between 1909 and 1911 Britain pressed for a reduction in German naval strength. Germany, on the other hand, demanded a promise of British neutrality in the event of an attack by France or Russia. The demands placed by each country on the other were impossible for either to accept and the gap could not be bridged. The Kaiser and Tirpitz did not seriously consider making any concessions over the fleet and Bethmann-Hollweg was only prepared to offer a slowing down in construction. Britain, in turn, viewed the German request for British neutrality as too high a price to pay. Both sides expected too much too soon. However, it was possible that with time the negotiations could have laid the basis for a better understanding. Instead, in 1911, Germany provoked another diplomatic crisis over Morocco. It began when Germany sought territorial compensation from the French Empire because the French had broken the Algeçiras agreement (see page 52). It developed into a major Anglo-German dispute because, in the face of what was regarded as German intimidation, Britain stood firmly by France, her *entente* partner. In this situation, the German government was not prepared to force the issue and risk war. Instead, she backed down and accepted a narrow strip of the French Congo as compensation. Little was gained by the episode and much was lost. As the political tension between Germany and Britain increased, the press in both countries stirred up hatred of each other and pressed for further increases in arms expenditure.

4 1911–14: The Last Years of Peace

> **KEY ISSUE** Did Germany intend to bring about a European war in 1914?

The last three years of peace have been the subject of much investigation by historians studying the causes of the First World War. Fischer maintains that the 'excitement and bitterness of nationalist opinion over what was seen to be the humiliating outcome of the (Moroccan) crisis were profound and enduring.' He argues that 1911 was an important year in German foreign policy because from that point there existed a clear continuity of German aims and policies that directly led to war in August 1914. Important to Fischer's view are the events of 1912. The Balkan Wars led to instability, particularly since Germany's main ally, Austria-Hungary, was threatened by an increasingly powerful and nationalistic Serbia backed by Russia. This fear of isolation and encirclement increased further when, following another failed attempt to find any basis for agreement, Germany had to watch while France and Britain carried out in-depth military conversations. Lord Haldane, the British war minister, who had once referred to Germany as 'his spiritual home' and was considered by some to have German sympathies, later told the German ambassador in London that Britain would stand by France unconditionally in the event of war. This was because Britain could not allow the balance of power in Europe to change in Germany's favour. The upshot of this was the calling of a meeting of Germany's army and navy chiefs on 8 December 1912. This meeting, which became known as the 'War Council' meeting, provides for the supporters of the Fischer view conclusive evidence of German intentions to fight a war at a time most suitable to German military interests. Other historians are not so sure. They have commented on the fact that the meeting 'amounted to almost nothing'. Attention has also been drawn to the informal nature of the meeting that was not even attended by Bethmann-Hollweg. Perhaps, the meeting was simply another example of a hasty response to an outburst by the Kaiser. It has also been questioned whether the chaotic nature of the German government was actually capable of such long-term planning.

By 1914, in Germany there was definitely a growing mood of pessimism and uncertainty about the future. The country had been drawn into an ever closer friendship with Austria-Hungary that increased the possibility of Germany being drawn into any Balkan conflict. The early months of 1914 witnessed a worsening in Russo-German relations. Some influential people in the German establishment held the belief that war provided the only escape from the looming crisis. However, in the last few months of peace Bethmann-Hollweg still saw hopeful signs in Germany's position. He was encouraged by the extent of Anglo-German co-operation during the Balkan Wars and by the peaceful settlement of several colonial disputes. To suggest that the evidence proves that the German government was actually planning a war in the summer of 1914 is to go too far. War plans certainly existed. The 'War Council' meeting of December 1912 is clear evidence of how war was considered to be a possible option. What it also reveals is that from 1912 German leaders were aware in their own minds of the extent to which, from a German point-of-view, 1914–15 was the most advantageous time for war. These considerations must surely have been very influential when the Sarajevo crisis (see page 56) developed. But this is not the same as claiming that Germany had decided to go to war whatever happened.

5 July 1914: Germany Goes to War

> **KEY ISSUE** Why did the situation in Europe deteriorate after the assassination of Archduke Franz Ferdinand?

This is not the place for a detailed account of the events across

Europe in the six weeks that followed the assassination of Archduke Franz Ferdinand in Sarajevo on 28 June 1914. Rather, it is more relevant to concentrate on what happened in Germany during this time. Following the assassination, Germany's first reaction was to give full backing to Austria-Hungary. This was done by offering Austria-Hungary unconditional support, the so-called 'blank cheque'. However, the German pressure for swift and decisive action combined with her knowledge of the severity of the ultimatum being prepared against Serbia suggests that she was taking more than just defensive measures on behalf of her ally. Bethmann-Hollweg seems to have recognised that the situation provided a fine opportunity for Austria to assert her power over Serbia in a localised war. An Austrian victory would also prove a significant diplomatic victory over Russia and over the *Entente* in general. Such a scheme was a gamble since there was a risk that Russia would stand by Serbia and thus broaden the conflict. In the first four weeks of July the German leaders seem to have been prepared to take that chance in the belief that Germany would win such a war. The diary of K. Riezler, secretary to Bethmann-Hollweg provides interesting reading:

1   7.7.1914... Our old dilemma in every Austrian move in the Balkans. If we encourage them, they will say we pushed them into it; if we try to dissuade them, then we're supposed to have left them in the lurch. Then they turn to the western powers whose arms are open, and we
5   lose our last halfway reliable ally. This time it's worse than 1912; for this time Austria is on the defensive against the subversive activities of Serbia and Russia. A move against Serbia can lead to world war.

23.7.1914... The Chancellor believes that if there is war it will be unleashed by Russian mobilisation ... In this case there will be little to
10 negotiate about because we shall have to wage war immediately in order to have a chance of winning. Yet, the entire nation will then sense the danger and rise in arms.

At this stage Germany did not necessarily want war, but it certainly seems to have been prepared to risk it.

a) The Serbian crisis of July 1914

The Austrian ultimatum to Serbia on 23 July brought home to the major powers the danger that had arisen because of the crisis. Britain, in particular, tried to mediate by calling for an international conference, but Germany ignored such proposals. Privately she urged Austria-Hungary to take military action because 'any delay in commencing military operations is regarded as a great danger because of the interference of other powers'. It would seem therefore that until 27 July there was a reasonable degree of agreement amongst the German leaders, but afterwards doubts began to appear amongst some of the leading figures and there were disagreements over policy.

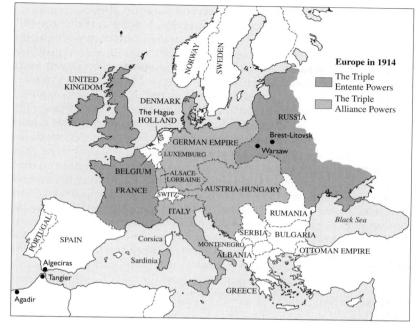

Europe in 1914

The Kaiser returned from his holiday on 28 July and proposed that the Austrians should 'halt in Belgrade' and then negotiate on the basis of the Serbian reply to the Austrian ultimatum. On the other hand, Moltke, the German Chief of Staff, was pressing his opposite number in Vienna to mobilise and prepare for an immediate war. The confusion brought about by such conflicting advice was hardly clarified by Bethmann-Hollweg. He was either playing a cunning diplomatic game to win over German public opinion to support a war by making Germany appear an innocent party in the face of Russian aggression or he too was hesitating and having doubts about the wisdom of taking such great risks. The Austrian declaration of war on Serbia on 28 July was followed by a Russian decision to order general mobilisation on 31 July. On the previous day, Bethmann-Hollweg had stated at a meeting that 'things are out of control and the stone has started to roll'. The crisis had gone beyond a situation where diplomacy was the most important to one where military matters came first. In Germany this was reflected by the increasing influence of the generals. Erich von Falkenhayn, the war minister, had already tried unsuccessfully to force Bethmann-Hollweg into ordering a mobilisation alert. Moltke also deliberately deceived his own government by urging Austria-Hungary to order general mobilisation against Russia although it had been previously agreed to allow Russia another 24 hours to back down. The point here is that Moltke and the generals not only saw the summer of 1914 as a best opportunity for war, but they also recognised that once Russia had mobilised, Germany would be committed to fight. This would bring into play a plan drawn up by Moltke's predecessor, Alfred von Schlieffen. The plan was intended to deal with the possibility of having to wage war on two fronts simultaneously – against Russia, in the east, and France, in the west. The plan involved an all-out assault in the west in order to defeat France before Russia could mobilise. Once France had been defeated, the German armies could turn east to face the Russians. Clearly, once Russia began to mobilise, Germany had no time to lose in preparing her own forces. The diplomatic gamble had failed and Bethmann-Hollweg recognised what now had to be done. War was declared on Russia on 1 August and against France, two days later, on 3 August. By this time there was no hope of Britain remaining neutral. The British ambassador and foreign secretary had both made it clear in the last few days of July that it was not in Britain's interests to stand aside and allow Germany to dominate Europe. Although at home there was some divided opinion over her entry into the war, Britain had guaranteed Belgian neutrality. The prospect of that country being invaded as part of the Schlieffen Plan made it almost certain that Britain would also be drawn into war with Germany.

6 Conclusion: The War – Who was Responsible?

Whilst Fischer's interpretation of German foreign policy has been very influential, his views have not been without their critics. For example, while some German historians do not deny that Germany was responsible for starting the war, the view of German structuralists is that domestic pressures in 1913–14 and not foreign policy decisions were the main reason why Germany went to war. The financial difficulties, the growing political power of the Social Democrats and the Zabern Affair are all seen as contributing to an internal crisis which encouraged the German elites to pursue a war policy as a means of side-tracking the political opposition and thereby preserving their own threatened position. This is generally referred to as the 'escape forwards' theory. Some critics have gone even further and suggested that Germany was ungovernable and that it had become affected by so many influences, many of which counteracted each other, that making policy decisions became an impossibility.

The inter-war view of German policy in 1914 as one of a defensive war against the *Entente* powers is now not generally accepted and some historians have continued to criticise Fischer for over-emphasising Germany's aggressive intentions. However, it has been suggested quite persuasively that German actions in 1914 represented 'an offensively conducted defensive war' by Germany – quite simply a view based on the idea held by some that attack is the best form of defence. In other words, it was an attempt to break free from the pressures brought about by isolation and the threatening power of Russia. As 1914 recedes further into the past the debate about the causes of the war becomes less blurred by the question of guilt. Younger generations detached from the horrors of two world wars have less reason to search for scapegoats. Germany and Britain are now partners in the European Union. However, the giving of historical explanations cannot avoid allocating responsibility, whether it is placed on individuals or nations.

Clearly, one cannot ignore the condition of Europe at the turn of the century. Powerful forces – technological, economic, ideological and those to do with population growth – were at work which helped to shape the international situation that made war possible. However, to emphasise the importance of such long-term factors is close to suggesting that war in 1914 was somehow inevitable. As the historian J. Röhl has written:

1 To argue that an event had deep causes and profound consequences is
   surely not to say that the deep causes were sufficient in themselves to
   bring about the event. It is my belief that the deeper causes ... were
   necessary, certainly, to produce the kind of war which broke out in
5 1914, but that those deeper factors (which had after all been present in
   the European situation for several decades prior to the outbreak of
   war) did not lead by themselves to a self-activation of war. The deeper
   causes were necessary but not sufficient. What is still missing is the
   decision-making dimension.

When one looks at the evidence from this level, it is difficult to escape from the conclusion that the German leadership must shoulder the major responsibility for both the worsening international climate in the five years before 1914 and also for turning the July crisis of 1914 into a European war. You will be aware from this chapter that German *Weltpolitik* and the ham-fisted diplomacy that accompanied it contributed to an increase in international tension and, by 1907, to a deterioration in Germany's position. Significantly, in the following years there was no real attempt by Germany to overcome this. There was no willingness to compromise as a way to encourage conciliation, trust and improve the prospects for peace. Instead, German foreign policy was generally of a warmongering type that was prepared to take risks. In part, this was made necessary by Germany's determination to stand by her one remaining reliable ally, Austria-Hungary. This policy and approach came to a head in the German response to events in the crisis of July 1914. From early July, Bethmann-Hollweg chose a policy that involved taking calculated risks in the hope of winning a diplomatic victory that would decisively weaken the *Entente*. To this end, the crisis was deliberately worsened and attempts at constructive mediation were impeded. All this was done because it was also believed that the failure of diplomacy would lead to a war with the *Entente* powers, which, according to the view of the generals, Germany could win. Thus, when Russia did mobilise in July 1914, Germany willingly accepted the challenge, declared war on Russia and France and began to implement the Schlieffen Plan.

Working on Chapter 4

In studying this chapter you will have become aware of the many different interpretations of the causes of the First World War. The question of responsibility for the war has long been disputed and there are almost as many differing views as there are historians. Which of the views is the most valid? Can the blame be fairly placed on Germany alone? The issue is pertinent since, at Versailles in 1919, the Allies forced German delegates to accept a War Guilt Clause and so accept total responsibility. As you have read, the German historian, Fritz Fischer is of the view that Germany's expansionist intentions were entirely to blame. Another German historian, Gerhard Ritter sees Germany as only party to blame. Was the First World War then simply the consequence of *Weltpolitik* or was it the result of the fact that German politicians needed to divert attention from the country's domestic problems? Is it possible that Lloyd George was correct when he said that the major European powers simply 'slithered over the brink into the boiling cauldron of war'?

These questions are ones for which you must have answers at your fingertips before sitting your examination. One very good way of sorting out your ideas about these issues is to discuss them with fellow students. But, in the end, you will definitely need to write brief answers to these questions for yourself. Now would be the best time to do this. If you wait till revision time there is a danger that you will not be able to allow yourself sufficient thinking time.

Source-based questions on Chapter 4

1. 'Few historical issues have been subject to such detailed analysis as the outbreak of the First World War. Colonial and economic rivalries, national pride and the armaments race have all been suggested as causes ... All these had added to the air of tension, yet none of them can be seen to have been particularly decisive in 1914. Indeed, the settlement of disputes by peaceful means had been one of the most remarkable achievements of the period; nor can economic factors be used to account for the military conflict. In fact, the immediate political circumstances point to the fundamental cause. That was that Serb nationalism could not live with Austria-Hungary and the Austrians resolved to crush Serbia whilst they had the support of Germany. Certainly there were wild elements in Serbia; the assassination of Franz Ferdinand was, from a European point of view, an act of utmost folly ... Beyond this, the fate of Europe had become bound up in the workings of rival alliances. Local war could only be prevented from becoming a wider one if one of the two groups was prepared to give way and this neither would do. A consequence of Germany's diplomatic arrogance in the previous years had been to leave her utterly dependent on her alliance with Austria-Hungary, a crucial factor, since the Austrian policy might well have been different without the support of Germany.'

(*Europe 1815–1945* by Anthony Wood, 1964)

a) Explain what is meant by i) 'all these added to the air of tension' and ii) 'there were wild elements in Serbia'. (*2 × 2 = 4 marks*)
b) What information can be inferred from the source about Austro-German relations during this period? (*6 marks*)
c) To what extent had the European powers been able to settle disputes by peaceful means during this period? (*8 marks*)
d) How useful is the source to an understanding of the extent of German responsibility for outbreak of war in 1914? (To answer the question use your own relevant background knowledge as well as the information provided in the source.) (*12 marks*)

2. SOURCE A.

ı German policy towards Morocco encompassed both colonial and European policy. It was therefore an essential part of *Weltpolitik*... In the *Entente Cordiale* of 1904 the British had recognised French interests in Morocco... Bulow and Holstein (the German foreign minister), initially
5 without the Kaiser's approval, saw Morocco as a means of testing the loyalty of the British to their new friend, France. Would Britain support France when Germany challenged her rights to influence in Morocco?
(*Years of Change. Europe 1890–1945* by Robert Wolfson and John Laver 1996)

SOURCE B.

ı The Kaiser, having agreed to disembark in Tangier, characteristically overplayed his part. Mounted on a splendid horse, to the accompaniment of a military band, the Kaiser rode through the streets of Tangier to the German legation. There he declared to the Sultan's representa-
5 tive and the assembled diplomatic corps that he hoped that independent Morocco would be open to trade with all countries. For the benefit of the French representatives, he added that he knew how to safeguard Germany's interests...
(*The First Morocco Crisis* by D.C. Watt, 1968 [adapted])

SOURCE C.

ı The German foreign secretary saw the chance to put pressure on France and the other members of the *Entente*... On 1 July 1911, a

German gunboat, the *Panther*, with 150 men arrived off the port of Agadir to 'protect' Germans living there. Some days later the German
5 government announced that, in return for recognising French control of Morocco, it wanted the French Congo... The British government warned Germany that no changes should be made without consulting Britain first. The British fleet prepared for action and plans were made
10 to mobilise 170,000 troops... Wilhelm was alarmed by the international storm and ordered his ministers to make smaller demands on France.
(*Bismarck, the Kaiser and Germany* by B.J. Elliott, 1972)

SOURCE D.

A German cartoon of 1911 shows Kaiser Wilhelm's mailed fist firmly implanted on Agadir.

a) Compare Sources B and C. How do the two sources contrast in their description of the Kaiser's approach to Morocco? (*5 marks*)
b) Study Sources A and D. How reliable are these sources as evidence to an historian of German aims in Morocco? (*5 marks*)
c) How useful are the sources to an understanding of events in Morocco in 1905 and 1911? (To answer the question use your own relevant background knowledge as well as the information provided by the sources.) (*10 marks*)

5 Germany and the First World War, 1914–18

POINTS TO CONSIDER

There is now little doubt amongst historians that the effects of the First World War were of great significance to the future history of Germany. The war acted as the stimulus for change. Germany entered the First World War still largely under the personal rule of the Kaiser; four years later, following humiliating defeat at the hands of the Allies, the Kaiser abdicated and fled to Holland. The *Kaiserreich* gave way to a democracy, the Weimar Republic. As you read this chapter for the first time you need to think about two questions: 1) Why did Imperial Germany fail to achieve the expected victory in the war? 2) In what ways did the four years of war affect the country?

KEY DATES

1914 War declared
Battle of Mons
Battle of the Marne
1915 Italy joined the Allies
Dardanelles campaign
Unrestricted submarine warfare began
1916 Battle of Verdun
Battle of the Somme
1917 United States entered the war
Michaelis replaced Bethmann-Hollweg as Chancellor
Revolution in Russia
1918 Failure of final German offensive
Treaty of Brest–Litovsk
Armistice signed

1 The Opening Moves

> **KEY ISSUE** How significant was the failure of the Schlieffen Plan to German plans in 1914?

a) The failure of the Schlieffen Plan

It is tempting to suggest that Germany's eventual military defeat in autumn 1918 is a good example of how one factor can prove decisive

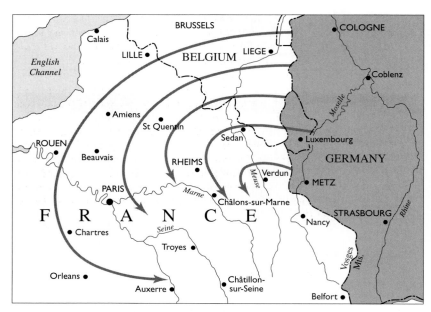

Schlieffen's original plan.

in deciding the outcome of a major on-going event such as a war. For in this case it seems that Germany's inability to achieve a quick victory in the autumn of 1914 resulted in a lengthy war for which the country was militarily and economically unprepared. Germany's military leaders had long recognised the weakness of Germany's position if faced by a combined attack on both western and eastern fronts. The Schlieffen Plan, named after a former German Chief of the General Staff, had been deliberately planned as a means of dealing with such a possibility.

1 In simple terms, the plan involved a surprise move in the west through Belgium and Luxembourg so as to encircle Paris and the French fortress towns close to the Franco-German frontier. It was hoped that this would bring about the defeat of France within six weeks. This would

5 then enable the transfer of German troops to the east to face the Russian armies which, because of the state's backwardness, it was thought would take a long time to mobilise. Although attractive in theory, the final draft of the plan produced by Schlieffen in 1905 was flawed in a number of ways. In order to advance on a broad front the

10 plan would need to violate the neutrality of Belgium, the Netherlands and Luxembourg without regard to the possible political consequences of such actions. This was yet another indication of the dominating influence of the military in the decision-making process of imperial

Germany. In addition, the plan was made at a time when Tsarist Russia
15 had political and military difficulties and consequently it was assumed
that Russian mobilisation would be slow. However, would this be true
of the future? There were also other considerations. Schlieffen's successor, Moltke, made a number of changes to the plan. The proposed
advance through the Netherlands was abandoned to prevent the risk of
20 any Dutch involvement in the war and because of concern about the
strength of the likely French assault in Alsace-Lorraine, some forces
were moved to the south. Whether the effects of these changes were
decisive in the failure of the plan has long been disputed. What does
seem clear is that, even before the first shots had been fired, the mili-
25 tary odds were not in Germany's favour. The Schlieffen Plan did not
provide any guarantee of success, and yet its failure was likely to draw
Germany into a war the outcome of which its own generals knew
would be highly doubtful.

b) The declaration of war

Wilhelm II's Proclamation of 6 August 1914:

1 To the German People

Ever since the foundation of our empire it has been the greatest
endeavour for me and for my forefathers over the last 43 years to preserve peace in the world and to continue our powerful development in
5 peace. But our enemies envy the success of our work. All the open and
secret hostility from east and west and from beyond the sea we have
endured conscious of our responsibility and power. But now these enemies want to humiliate us. They wish us to look on with folded arms as
they prepare a malicious attack; they do not tolerate our standing side
10 by side in determined loyalty with our allies who fight for their reputa-
tions as empires and with their humiliation we will lose our power and
honour as well. Therefore the sword must now decide. In the midst of
peace the enemy attacks us. Forward. To arms. Every moment of
wavering, every hesitation is treason against the Fatherland. The exist-
15 ence or destruction of our re-created empire is now at stake, the very
existence of German power and customs. We will resist to the last
breath of air of man and horse. And we will win this fight even against
a world of enemies. Germany has never lost when it has been united.
Forward with God who will be with us as He was with our fathers.

20 Berlin. 6 August 1914. Wilhelm.

2 The Course of the War

> **KEY ISSUE** How successful were the alternative strategies used by the Germans in an effort to win the war?

a) Stalemate on the Western Front

The optimism of August 1914 soon disappeared as the Germans came face to face with the realities of the military situation. Russia mobilised more quickly than expected and in desperation Moltke transferred additional German army units to the Eastern Front. The main offensive meanwhile came up against Belgian resistance that was stiffer than expected and this was soon to be reinforced by the arrival of British troops, the British Expeditionary Force or BEF. Even so, in late August, following the Battle of Mons, the British were forced to retreat but, as the German lines of communication lengthened, so the speed of their advance slowed. Moltke then decided not to encircle Paris but to move to the east of the French capital. This exposed his flank to a counter attack and, in September 1914, at the Battle of the Marne the Germans were forced to retreat to the River Aisne. The Schlieffen Plan had failed. Moltke suffered a nervous breakdown and resigned and was replaced by Erich von Falkenhayn. Admittedly, on the Eastern Front the Germans had gained a couple of memorable victories against Russia, but that country was still very much in the war and a very real threat to Austria-Hungary, Germany's major ally.

The implications of Germany's inability to gain the intended quick victory were far-reaching. By November 1914 Germany was confronted with a war on two fronts. This was a situation that it had always wished to avoid and for which it was not prepared militarily, or economically. The generals had long recognised the dangers of such a situation, but in the end their plan had been unable to prevent it. If Germany were to win the war, it had to develop a workable alternative strategy.

b) The failure of alternative strategies

Throughout 1915 Germany struggled to come up with an appropriate long-term strategy to overcome the unexpected military stalemate. Victories on the Eastern Front against Russia and the withdrawal of the Allies from the Dardanelles campaign could not alter the fact that time was against Germany. The Allies had already gained the maritime advantage by seizing German colonies and destroying its roving cruisers that had successfully preyed on unarmed British merchant vessels. Most significantly, Britain had imposed a naval blockade which severely limited Germany's ability to import essential foodstuff and raw materials. The German response to this threat is telling evidence of the leadership's inability to develop a co-ordinated and purposeful strategy. Although Admiral Tirpitz wanted to engage the British fleet in battle in order to break the blockade, other voices felt that this was far too dangerous since it risked the loss of the German High Seas Fleet. As an alternative, Tirpitz consequently pressed for the use of unrestricted submarine warfare, the sinking of all ships bound for Britain irrespective of their nationality. This too led to fierce controversy. There were doubts about the morality, as well as the effectiveness of the policy. Bethmann-Hollweg was also rightly aware of the possible diplomatic consequences for the neutral USA. However, the Chancellor accepted military advice and in February 1915 unrestricted submarine warfare was introduced. It was short lived and, following the sinking of the liner *Lusitania* in September with the the loss of 1,098 lives, 128 of them Americans, it was brought to an end. In February 1916 the policy was re-adopted only to be dropped again within a few weeks when the USA threatened to break off diplomatic relations. At this point Tirpitz resigned. Such inconsistency was a sign of the divisions and uncertainties within the German leadership about how the war could be brought to a successful conclusion.

The limitations of German planning were further revealed in 1916. Falkenhayn believed that the war could only be won on the Western Front and to this end his plan to launch a massive assault against the key French fortress town of Verdun was accepted. His declared aim was to 'bleed the French army white on the anvil of Verdun'. The casualties on both sides were horrifying but the French held on. The failure at Verdun along with the losses suffered in the Battle of the Somme, fought later in the same year, undermined Falkenhayn's position completely and he was replaced in the summer of 1916 by the joint leadership of Paul von Hindenburg and Erich Ludendorff.

During the years 1915–16 Germany had been unable to break the deadlock created by the failure of the Schlieffen Plan. Alternative strategies either lacked imagination or were pursued without real commitment. As one historian has put it: 'What they [the Germans] could not do was escape from the remorseless logic of a two-front war'. As victory failed to materialise the economic pressures of conflict grew more intense.

3 The Home Front

> **KEY ISSUE** What measures did the Germans adopt in order to cope with shortages on the home front?

a) Germany's economic limitations

Germany's economic growth was the foundation stone of its emergence as a world power in the years before 1914 (see pages 9–12). Such economic strength was dependent above all on Germany's ability to trade. However, the imposition of the blockade and the demands of a long drawn out war created enormous economic strains. Germany's banks and export industries were badly disrupted, whilst Germany's ability to import foodstuffs and raw materials was severely curtailed. Some items, such as oil, rubber, nitrates and the metals copper and mercury, were vital to war production. Others, such as fats and fertilisers were essential if Germany's population was to be adequately fed. Of course, Germany was not alone in experiencing such problems, but surrounded by enemies, her circumstances meant that the situation was more difficult. Therefore, success in the war necessitated the total mobilisation of the nation's economy.

b) Mobilising the economy for the needs of war

The urgency of the situation was soon recognised. Walther Rathenau, the owner of Germany's largest electricity company, worked to create the *Kriegsrohstoffabteilung*, known as the KRA (War Raw Materials Department), within the War Ministry. The KRA oversaw a range of companies whose job it was to acquire, store and distribute the most vital raw materials in the interests of the war effort. Such direct government intervention was most clearly shown over the shortage of nitrates. These were central to the manufacture of explosives. The KRA not only established a chemicals section, but also backed the construction of several plants to produce nitrates by an artificial process. Within six months the KRA had successfully organised the provision of most essential supplies and prevented the looming munitions crisis.

State intervention also became increasingly apparent in other fields. Labour was affected by the role of the War Ministry in deciding who should be conscripted and who exempted from military service. There was also the need to prevent industrial unrest. This led to the creation of local War Boards made up of representatives of management and labour. There were also attempts to control consumption by means of rationing and price controls and so ensure a fair distribution of scarce goods. For example, early in 1915 bread rationing was introduced and by the end of 1916 it had been extended to all foodstuffs. Even so, as we shall see, there was still discontent amongst the civilian population.

In the short term, the measures taken by the German leadership to regulate the war economy were reasonably successful. However, military victory was not forthcoming in 1915–16. As a result, two important economic weaknesses continued to reduce Germany's capacity to maintain her fighting capacity. These were the government budget and the provision of food. Germany had already been running a massive government debt in peace-time, and it saw it increase rapidly once the war started. The sale of war bonds represented the only real

German posters of the First World War. (right) Germanica appears above the slogan 'God punish England'; (left) a poster of 1917 uses a submarine to encourage Germans to buy War Loan bonds.

attempt to narrow the gap between income and expenditure. The idea of raising taxes on income and industrial profits, the burden of which would have fallen mainly on the rich, was rejected on political grounds. The cost of the war was simply put off until the end of the war when compensation in the form of reparations could be demanded from the defeated countries. Altogether, only 16 per cent of the cost of the war was met from taxation. Such a massive expansion of the amount of money in circulation not only fuelled inflation within Germany, but also reduced the value of the mark internationally. Even more disturbing was Germany's inability to feed itself. The effects of the blockade and the conscription of so many able-bodied males who had formerly worked on the land led to a decline in grain production. However, attempts to establish government control over the agricultural landowners were unsuccessful. Eventually, a War Nutrition Office was set up to regulate food supplies, but it met massive resistance from the powerful agricultural lobby and its measures proved inadequate. Production continued to decline and, because insufficient food was made available at the regulated prices, a black market flourished. In this, goods were sold contrary to the regulations to those able to afford high prices. By the end of 1916 the economic situation was such that the Supreme Army Command determined to intensify the war effort by a clearly defined set of targets. The Hindenburg Programme aimed to increase arms production massively by placing contracts directly with heavy industry, whilst the introduction of the Auxiliary Service Law was supposed to achieve 'the mobilisation of the entire civilian population for war service'. In fact, both ideas fell short of their objectives and problems of labour and production continued to hinder the German war effort.

The onset of 'total war', a war that spared neither the military nor the civilian population, forced Germany to use the power of the state as a means of mobilising its economic potential. However, there were limits on how far this policy could go because of the reaction of certain key interest groups. Ironically, autocratic Germany failed to achieve the same degree of mobilisation as in democratic Britain where war-time agreement amongst the civilian population proved to be more productive in the long run. In Germany, the First World War did not result in a state controlled economy, government financial policy was unchanged, industries were not nationalised, and the property rights of landowners were left relatively untouched. In this sense the German economy was never fully mobilised to meet the military demands of the situation. Yet, as we will see, the consequences of this economic policy were to be disastrous in the long term for the stability of the *Kaiserreich,* since the political blame for the nation's problems was increasingly laid on the state.

4 The Latter Stages of the War, 1917–18

> **KEY ISSUE** In what sense was the German declaration of
> unrestricted submarine warfare in 1917 a gamble?

a) Submarine warfare and the entry of the USA

Although Hindenburg and Ludendorff were determined to pursue
the war with the utmost vigour and to reject any possibility of a negotiated peace, they were unable to offer any new military strategy.
There was no way out of the deadlock on the Western Front and the
passage of time simply played further into the hands of the Allies. It
was this dilemma which encouraged the military to press once again
for the introduction of unrestricted submarine warfare in the belief
that this would bring Britain to its knees. Bethmann-Hollweg
remained unconvinced by this 'miracle cure' and its possible side
effects. Even so, by January 1917 he had become unpopular and was
politically too isolated to offer effective opposition to the plan. The
following month a new submarine campaign was launched. Within a
few months the futility of the policy was only too apparent.
Admittedly, Britain initially suffered catastrophic losses, but the
introduction of the convoy system during the latter half of 1917
proved decisive in reducing the losses to tolerable levels and by 1918
it was clear that the Germans were losing the submarine war. More
significantly, it proved a major contributory factor in the American
decision to enter the war in April 1917. The military situation was now
stacked against Germany. The resources of the world's greatest economic power – finance, industry and manpower – were mobilised in
the interests of the Allies whilst the economic strains on Germany and
the Central Powers continued to increase.

b) 1918 The failure of the German final offensive

As 1917 drew to a close, Germany's defeat seemed only a matter of
time. The fact that Germany did not actually surrender until
November 1918 was mainly due to events in Russia. There revolution
and the establishment of the Bolshevik regime in November 1917
resulted in Russia seeking an armistice with Germany followed by a
negotiated peace in March 1918, the Treaty of Brest–Litovsk. These
events provided a new opportunity for the German leadership. Not
only did they boost civilian and military morale at a critical time, but
it also freed Germany from the two-front war and opened up the
chance to snatch victory by concentrating German military might on
the Western Front. However, although Germany's intended victory
offensive in the west, often referred to as Ludendorff's final offensive, at first made considerable progress, the Allied lines were never

decisively broken and the offensive slowly ground to a halt. There were several reasons for this. Ironically, the German high command still kept one and a half million men on the Eastern Front to establish and maintain control over the territory gained by the Treaty of Brest–Litovsk. Such numbers could have provided vital reserves to maintain the momentum of advance during the offensive on the Western Front. Instead, German troops on the Western Front were faced by ever increasing numbers of American troops. These men were fresh and had not been subjected to the demoralising effects of trench warfare over the previous three years. When the Allies counter-attacked in August, German troops proved incapable of withstanding the assault, although their retreat remained an orderly one. By mid-September, the final German defensive positions, the Hindenburg Line, had been broken and the western region of Germany faced the very real possibility of invasion. In the south-east of Europe, Germany's allies, Turkey, Bulgaria, and Austria-Hungary, all faced imminent collapse. Even Hindenburg and Ludendorff at last recognised the extent of the crisis and on 29 September they advised the Kaiser that Germany must sue for an armistice. The war had been lost.

c) Conclusion

With hindsight there appears to have been almost some inevitability about Germany's defeat in the First World War once the Schlieffen Plan failed to achieve the rapid victory that the German military leadership recognised as so vital. Yet, although logic suggested that a two-front war could not be won, the German leadership refused to accept the possibility of a negotiated peace. The surrender of Russia in early 1918 did briefly offer the possibility of an escape from 'the strategic strait-jacket'. Unfortunately, the German capacity to mobilise and maintain a major offensive in 1918, particularly in the face of the American entry into the war and the collapse of its own allies, was insufficient to affect the outcome. In addition, there were other reasons why Germany lost the war. Even before the American entry, the most important Allies, Britain and France, were major colonial powers and could call upon their overseas empires for material and manpower support. Whilst their own economic blockade of Britain had come close to bringing that country to its knees, in the end the Allied blockade of Germany, more easily achieved, was more decisive. Germany too was handicapped by having to support weak allies.

5 The Domestic Impact of War

> **KEY ISSUE** For what reasons did the military become increasingly involved in the economic and political affairs of the nation?

a) *Burgfriede*

Essentially, Germany went to war in August 1914 united in a patriotic fervour against what was perceived as the threat posed by 'barbaric Russia'. Numerous writers, who saw the war as a mixture of adventure and liberation, caught the mood of the moment. Bruno Frank's contemporary poem was typical:

1 Proud Times, 1914
   Rejoice, friends, that we are alive
   And that we're young and nimble!
   Never was there a year like this,
5 And never such a gift for youth!
   It is given to us to take our stand or to strike out
   Eastwards or westwards.
   The greatest of all of earth's ages
   Sets its brand upon our young hearts.

The view was reflected at a political level as well. A political truce, *Burgfriede*, was agreed between all the political parties and the necessary loans to finance the war were passed unanimously. Even the Social Democrats, who for so long had been viewed as unpatriotic pacifist 'enemies of the state', promised their support for a defensive war. Their attitude came as a surprise to many in the military that had been seriously considering the need to make mass arrests and to impose press censorship as a way of keeping them in check. However, such methods were not required for several reasons. Firstly, the party was taken in by the way the government successfully managed to portray the war as a defensive war. Secondly, many Social Democrats were naturally very patriotic and were genuinely proud of their country's achievements. This in turn led to a belief, particularly amongst the more moderate elements of the leadership, that by showing loyalty in the nation's hour of crisis the party could gain political recognition that in the long run would enhance the possibility of Germany becoming a truly democratic nation.

The failure to secure a quick victory and the onset of military stalemate by Christmas 1914 certainly did much to undermine the enthusiastic spirit of August 1914. However, critical views remained few in number during the first half of the war. Lulled into a false sense of security by the power of the military censors and government propaganda, the public mood remained confident of eventual victory. It was only during 1916, with the losses at Verdun and on the Somme,

An die deutschen Juden!

In schicksalsernster Stunde ruft das Vaterland seine Söhne unter die Fahnen.

Daß jeder deutsche Jude zu den Opfern an Gut und Blut bereit ist, die die Pflicht erheischt, ist selbstverständlich.

Glaubensgenossen! Wir rufen Euch auf, **über das Maß der Pflicht hinaus** Eure Kräfte dem Vaterlande zu widmen! Eilet freiwillig zu den Fahnen! Ihr alle — Männer und Frauen — stellt Euch durch persönliche Hilfeleistung jeder Art und durch Hergabe von Geld und Gut in den Dienst des Vaterlandes!

Berlin, den 1. August 1914.

Verband der Deutschen Juden.
Centralverein deutscher Staatsbürger jüdischen Glaubens.

An interesting press release of 1914 begins – 'TO GERMAN JEWS. In fateful hours, the Fatherland calls its sons to the colours. That every German Jew is ready as duty demands for sacrifice of life and wealth goes without saying. Fellow believers! We call upon you to give your all. . .'

that doubts began to be expressed about the way the war was going. The *Burgfriede* had lasted well over two years during which time the government had faced no real opposition from the public or the *Reichstag*. The debates were limited to the leadership, where individuals and factions competed to exert the greatest influence.

b) The 'Silent Dictatorship'

It has already been seen how Germany's military leaders supported intervention in the nation's economy on the grounds that it was necessary in order to win the war. However, as the war progressed the military leadership became increasingly involved in political affairs. Why was this?

Firstly, there was the position of the Kaiser himself. Whatever controversies may exist about the Kaiser's political influence in the pre-war years, there is little doubt that he exerted no real control over political and military affairs during the war. His self-confidence and determination, already badly shaken by *The Daily Telegraph* affair, seemed to desert him with the onset of war and all its accompanying problems. Despite being supreme warlord, he was kept in the dark about military developments and his advice was rarely sought. As a political leader he was no more than a figurehead and an increasingly distant one at that. He did not even make a serious attempt to project a propaganda image of himself as the caring leader of his people, preferring instead to while away his time on his estates. However, the impotence of the Kaiser also had important consequences for the power exerted by the Chancellor. Bethmann-Hollweg did not enjoy popular backing and the *Burgfriede* in the *Reichstag* was pursued because of patriotic loyalty, not out of respect for the Chancellor. All along, Bethmann-Hollweg's power base had been the support of the Kaiser and yet as the war progressed that support became increasingly unreliable. This left the Chancellor and his government increasingly isolated and incapable of resisting the interference of the military.

In the summer of 1916 the developing political crisis came to a head. By this time, of course, the military situation was a cause of grave concern and many conservatives looked to place the blame on Bethmann-Hollweg himself. The policy of unrestricted submarine warfare had already caused divisions between the government and the military, and Bethmann-Hollweg's abandonment of the policy for the second time was viewed with suspicion. Another cause of conservative resentment was the Chancellor's friendly approaches to the socialists of the SPD, which he felt were necessary in order to maintain their political support for the war. This ended with Bethmann-Hollweg successfully persuading the Kaiser to accept the need to reform Prussia's outdated voting system. This, in turn, made him conscious of the need to shore up his own political position by winning popular support. Therefore, he decided to ditch Falkenhayn and to replace him with the popular military hero Hindenburg, who had so successfully led the German forces on the Eastern Front. On 29 August 1916 Hindenburg and his deputy Ludendorff became joint leaders of the Supreme Military Command.

The emergence of Hindenburg and Ludendorff was indeed a turning point, but not in the way intended by Bethmann-Hollweg. Far from strengthening his position, the Chancellor soon found that the authority of both himself and the Kaiser had been seriously weakened. Neither of them enjoyed the popularity of Hindenburg and Ludendorff. Thus, by the simple means of threatening resignation, the High Command was able to exert a powerful influence over political, economic and military events. With the authority of the Emperor and the Chancellor so weakened, the two main props of the Bismarck's constitution had been undermined. To all intents and purposes effective power for the next two years lay with so-called 'silent dictatorship' of the supreme army command, the OHL. Several opportunities for a negotiated peace were turned down, on its instruction ministers were replaced and promoted and the Auxiliary Service Law was introduced to militarise society. Eventually, in July 1917, Hindenburg and Ludendorff forced the unfortunate Bethmann-Hollweg out of office. He had once again opposed the reintroduction of unrestricted submarine warfare, had raised the possibility of constitutional reform by establishing a special parliamentary committee to consider the issue and had failed to prevent the passage of the *Reichstag* peace resolution. Wilhelm was unwilling to let his Chancellor go, but he recognised where the real power now lay. Bethmann-Hollweg resigned and was succeeded by the virtually unknown Georg Michaelis who was described by one SPD deputy as – 'the fairy angel tied to the Christmas tree at Christmas for the children's benefit'.

In the last year of the war, the power of the supreme army command reached new heights. The constitutional authority of the Emperor and the Chancellor were effectively sidelined. Even the

Reichstag, having expressed its desire for peace, proved unable or unwilling to exert any further political pressure. Instead, the power of the army, which had been such a key feature of the *Kaiserreich* since its foundation, had, under the conditions of total war, eventually become obvious to everyone. The real masters of Germany were the 'silent dictators', Hindenburg and Ludendorff.

PAUL VON HINDENBURG (1847–1934) *-Profile-*

1847   born at Posen
1859   joined the Prussian army
1870   fought in the Franco-Prussian War. Awarded the Iron Cross
1873   appointed to General Staff
1911   retired with the rank of general
1914   recalled to the army and appointed supreme commander on the Eastern Front
1916   transferred to Western Front
1918   retired to his estate in East Prussia
1925   elected President of the Weimar Republic
1930   used presidential authority to rule by decree
1932   won re-election as President
1933   appointed Hitler Chancellor of Germany
1934   died

Hindenburg was born into a Prussian noble family that could trace its military tradition back over many centuries. Described as 'steady rather than exceptional', he was regularly promoted and, in 1914, his management of the campaign against the Russians on the Eastern Front earned him distinction. In fact, Hindenburg, who was distinguished in appearance and 'looked the part', did not have great military skills and was outshone by his chief-of-staff Ludendorff. After 1916, the partnership was less successful against the British and French on the Western Front. During the years 1917 and 1918, Hindenburg and Ludendorff were effectively the military dictators of Germany. After the war, Hindenburg briefly retired but in 1925 he was elected President of Germany, a position he held until 1934. In his mid-eighties, he was involved in the political intrigue that ended with Hitler being appointed Chancellor.

ERICH LUDENDORFF (1865–1937)

-*Profile*-

1865	born at Kruszewnia
1882	joined the Prussian army
1906	appointed chief of operations
1914	appointed chief-of-staff to Hindenburg on the Eastern Front
1916	transferred to Western Front
1917	responsible for dismissal of Bethmann-Holweg
1918	masterminded German final offensive
	fled to Sweden. Put forward 'stab in the back theory'
1919	returned to Germany
1920	took part in Kapp *putsch*
1923	collaborated with Hitler and was involved in Munich *putsch*
1937	died

Ludendorff didn't share the Hindenburg family's military background. As a result, he was commissioned into one of the less fashionable German foot regiments. However, his energy and enthusiasm soon earned him rapid promotion. His ability attracted the attention of both von Schlieffen and von Moltke and by the outbreak of war he was a brigade commander. In the campaign in Belgium he showed considerable initiative and was sent, as chief-of-staff, to serve with Hindenburg on the Eastern Front. Here he played an important part in the major victories gained against the Russians. In 1916, the two men were posted to the Western Front and during the years that followed they were able to assume supreme command of the German war effort. By the end of the war, Ludendorff was effectively the wartime dictator of Germany. After the war, he dabbled in extreme right-wing politics. He became associated with the activities of Hitler's Nazi Party whose racial views he shared. Later he became disenchanted with Hitler and in his latter years became a pacifist.

6 The Home Front – the Human Experience

> **KEY ISSUE** To what extent did the war affect the everyday lives of ordinary German people?

a) The impact of the war on civilian morale

For those directly involved, the First World War was unlike any previous conflict. It is hard to convey in words the real horrors of that war. Its impact upon millions of Germans was severe in the extreme. Germany's war dead totalled 2.4 million – 16 per cent of those conscripted. Millions more suffered permanent disabilities, both physical and mental. Of course, such statistics fail to convey the human and emotional consequences. Few families escaped the trauma of a death or a casualty. By 1918, a popular joke was circulating – 'What family is going to survive the war with all six sons alive?' The Kaiser had six sons and the joke was a bitter comment on Germany's human tragedy and the declining popularity of the royal family. Any assessment of the results of such war experiences is fraught with difficulty. It is easy to generalise and it would be easy to be wrong. Perhaps the safe conclusion is the most accurate one – different people were affected in different ways. Some soldiers serving in the trenches were drawn into left-wing politics in the hope of creating a socialist society after the war. Others, like Adolf Hitler, found the discipline and camaraderie

Indices of real wages 1913–19				
Year	Railwaymen	Printers	Miners	Civil Servants
1913	100.0	100.0	100.0	100.0
1914	97.2	97.2	93.3	97.2
1915	79.7	77.3	81.3	77.3
1916	69.2	60.6	74.4	58.9
1917	63.9	49.4	62.7	48.6
1918	83.9	54.1	63.7	55.0
1919	92.2	72.3	82.4	54.8

Strikes and lock-outs 1913–19		
Year	No. of strikes	No. of workers	Working days lost
1913	2,464	0.323m	11.76m
1915	141	0.015m	0.04m
1917	562	0.668m	1.86m
1919	3,719	2.132m	33.08m

of the trenches fulfilling and so turned their experiences of patriotism and death into heroic ideals they wished to transfer to post-war German society. Many more simply grew resentful of the sacrifices made whilst rumours circulated about the luxury and indulgence to be found behind the lines amongst the higher ranking officers. Within the ranks of the navy things were very different, since the lack of military action led to boredom and frustration. However, it should be noted that despite signs of resentment within the German military, there was no large scale break-down of discipline and order until the last few weeks of the war. Only when the war was lost and political change had begun did the discontent within the military combine with growing unrest within the civilian population.

b) Shortages

On the home front, the impact of war was great on the everyday lives of ordinary Germans. For the first two years the effects were generally those of inconvenience rather than real hardship but, by the autumn of 1916, the accumulation of shortages, the effects of high prices and

A cartoon of 1916 indicates that after two years of war the German people had not entirely lost their sense of humour. The caption reads – 'Look here, woman, we've been at war with each other for some twenty years – and all this fuss about just two years!'

the black market as well as the bleak military situation began to affect the public mood. Undoubtedly, the situation was worse in the towns than in the countryside, since farmers inevitably looked after their own interests first. For the town and city dwellers living standards were declining. Only those workers involved in the essential war industries were able to use their strong bargaining position and thereby avoid the shortages facing the rest. In the so-called 'turnip winter' of 1916–17, a time when the German population relied heavily on turnips which were not normally used for human consumption for their food, the situation deteriorated sharply. An exceptionally cold winter combined with a poor potato crop contributed to a disastrous food and fuel crisis. The following summer the cereal harvest fell to half that of 1913. As a result of the Auxiliary Service Law, many workers were forced to work even longer hours. Civilian deaths from starvation and hypothermia increased from 121,000 in 1916 to 293,000 in 1918, whilst infant mortality increased by over 50 per cent in the course of the war years.

In fact, as the American historian Volker Berghahn has written, 'the emergency of total war failed to create a genuine inter-class solidarity, but furthered group egotism' with the result that social discontent grew markedly. Considerable anger was expressed against the 'sharks' of industry who had made vast profits from the war. Resentment grew in the minds of many within the middle class because their income was declining and because they felt that their social status had been lowered. Above all, opposition began to grow against a political leadership that had urged total war, but seemed incapable of ensuring equality of sacrifice. Such hostility was further evident in the heated political debate over Germany's war aims.

7 Germany's War Aims

> **KEY ISSUE** To what extent did Germans agree on their war aims?

a) *Burgfriede* and *Siegfriede*

The issue of war aims was central to the political and economic changes taking place in wartime Germany and it went beyond a debate over mere territorial gains. It also directly concerned the question of what kind of Germany was to exist after the war. For this reason Bethmann-Hollweg was keen to avoid a public debate on war aims. He saw the maintenance of the *Burgfriede* as essential and he feared that discussion of war aims would cause arguments at home and damage Germany's status, especially among neutral powers, abroad.

Bethmann-Hollweg's problem was that once the military stalemate had set in by 1915, two very different versions of the future peace began to emerge in Germany. On the one hand, there were those who believed that Germany was fighting a purely defensive war and not one aimed at conquest. This view was most clearly expressed within the ranks of the SPD, which upheld that the peace should be based upon compromise, reconciliation and no territorial gains. On the other hand, there were those who argued for a *Siegfriede*, a peace of victory, by which Germany would use its position of strength to win control over Europe and thus finally achieve its long-cherished world-power status. *Siegfriede* found expression in its most extreme form in the programme of the Pan-German League. The League stood for the creation of a Central African empire, the annexation of key military and industrial regions in Holland, Belgium and northern France, the economic domination of western Europe in the interests of Germany, and the annexation of extensive territories in the east from Russia. Moreover, such ideas were not limited to a lunatic fringe of the extreme conservative right wing. The basic ideas of the *Siegfriede* were widely supported by other political parties and different social classes. All the main parties, with the exception of the SPD, supported some version of peace with territorial gains. This, in turn, reflected the growth in influence of such views amongst broad sections of the middle class as well as the upper class. However, this was not just a case of nationalists wanting territorial gains, it was an outcome of the fear that unless Germany achieved a decisive victory with territorial gains and compensation from the defeated countries, it would prove impossible to prevent the existing condition in Germany from undergoing great change. In this sense the pursuit of the *Siegfriede* was seen as essential in order to maintain the existing system at home. A peace aimed at the reconciliation would only encourage internal changes and reform.

The emergence of these two conflicting viewpoints in the course of 1915 created all sorts of problems for a Chancellor who desired to maintain a united political front in the *Reichstag* and in the nation at large. His own personal sympathies were undoubtedly with some kind of *Siegfriede*, although he was astute enough to recognise the dangers of expressing this openly. For this reason, Bethmann-Hollweg's September Programme of 1914, which outlined specific German annexations in the west, the desirability of ending Russian influence on Germany's eastern frontier and finally the need to create a German-dominated European economic association, always remained a secret and it never became official government policy. The Chancellor worked hard to avoid creating divisions, but the worsening social and military situation from the middle of 1916 only served to increase the agitation and highlight the divisions over war aims. In 1917 it became impossible for him to continue with his middle of the road stance as the pressure increased from both the left and the right. The growing political interference of the High Command totally undermined his hope of negotiating peace with

Russia and the USA. In April 1917 he felt obliged to endorse the *Kreuznach* Programme of the military. This was a list of war aims that included territorial gains in both east and west as well as the extension of German economic rights. Although the Chancellor claimed that this document would not stand in his way if a genuine chance of a negotiated peace came along, it was clear that his room for manoeuvre was running out. His apparent support for the *Kreuznach* Programme inevitably reduced further his standing with the non-conservative forces on the left. The political situation was further changed by the revolutionary overthrow of the Tsar in Russia. This led to a split in the SPD that saw the emergence of a more extreme Independent Social Democratic Party (USPD) wholly committed to bringing about a speedy end to the war.

b) The peace resolution

When in July 1917 Matthias Erzberger, the voice of the Centre, suggested peace without territorial gains, there emerged a coalition of forces in the *Reichstag* willing to support his idea. The motion stated:

> 'The *Reichstag* strives for a peace of understanding and permanent reconciliation of peoples. Forced territorial acquisitions and political, economic and financial oppressions are irreconcilable with such a peace'.

The peace resolution was passed by 212 votes to 126.

Although Bethmann-Hollweg resigned, nothing was really achieved by the peace resolution. The *Reichstag* did not seize the opportunity to press its own claims to political authority or to demand negotiations for peace. Equally, the High Command did not change its policy. Indeed, the appointment of Michaelis as Chancellor merely served to strengthen further the political hold of Hindenburg and Ludendorff who rejected out of hand anything less than the *Kreuznach* Programme. To this end, the OHL was instrumental a few months later in the creation of the *Vaterlandspartei,* the Fatherland Party. This deliberately set out to mobilise mass support behind the military by politically supporting the demands of the extreme right wing. Led by Tirpitz and financially backed by some leading industrialists, it proved remarkably successful. By 1918 it boasted 1.2 million members.

The creation of the *Vaterlandspartei* and the passage of the peace resolution shows how Germany had become divided into two increasingly hostile camps. Those who called for a compromise peace without forced annexations were mainly the supporters of constitutional reform. Those who backed the Fatherland Party wanted the political situation to remain as it was.

At the beginning of 1918 it seemed as if the forces of conservatism would emerge supreme. The Treaty of Brest–Litovsk represented a decisive victory for the supporters of *Siegfriede*. A *Siegfriede* on this scale

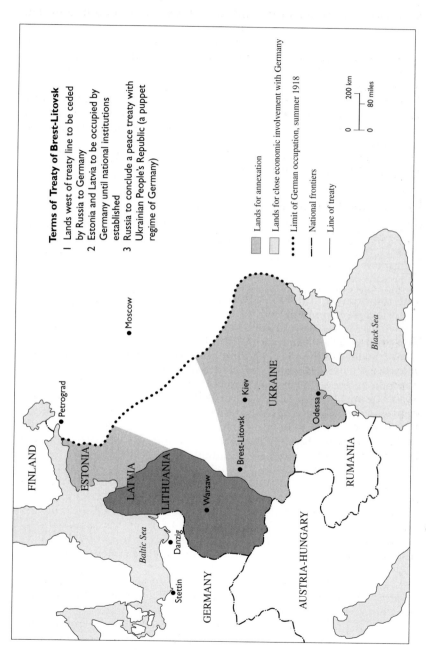

Terms of Treaty of Brest-Litovsk

1 Lands west of treaty line to be ceded by Russia to Germany

2 Estonia and Latvia to be occupied by Germany until national institutions established

3 Russia to conclude a peace treaty with Ukrainian People's Republic (a puppet regime of Germany)

Lands for annexation

Lands for close economic involvement with Germany

••••• Limit of German occupation, summer 1918

—·— National frontiers

——— Line of treaty

0   200 km
0   80 miles

German influence in Eastern Europe after the Treaty of Brest-Litovsk (1918)

not only liberated Germany from the two-front war and made victory in the west now possible, it also greatly strengthened the political standing of the military leadership. The *Reichstag* backed the treaty by a large majority and only the USPD voted against it. However, there were already widespread strikes in Germany's major cities in early 1918. The High Command remained seemingly unconcerned about the implications of the industrial action and placed a blind faith in victory in the west and the imposition of another *Siegfriede*. Thus, when the hoped-for military victory did not materialise, a revolutionary situation emerged. In a letter to a friend written on 21 October 1918 Meinecke stated:

1   A fearful and gloomy existence awaits us in the best of circumstances! And although my hatred of the enemy, who remind me of beasts of prey, is as hot as ever, so is my anger and resentment at those German power politicians who, by their presumption and their stupidity, have 5   dragged us down into this abyss. Repeatedly in the course of the war, we could have had a peace by agreement, if it had not been that boundless demands of the Pan-German-militaristic-conservative combine made it impossible. It is fearful and tragic that this combine could be broken only by the overthrow of the whole state.

The importance of the First World War in shaping Germany's future historical development cannot be over-emphasised. A German military victory in 1918 would almost certainly have defused the crisis and in so doing slowed the process of political reform for a generation or more. Instead, four years of total war ending in defeat brought the *Kaiserreich* to its knees. It had a dramatically adverse effect on the German economy by further damaging the government's already difficult financial position. This, in turn, was to lead to run-away inflation and the severe strains that this placed on the German economy and German society. In pre-war Germany there had been instability and the occasional political crises. By the autumn of 1918, Germany found herself in a revolutionary situation.

Summary Diagram
Germany in War and Revolution, 1914–19

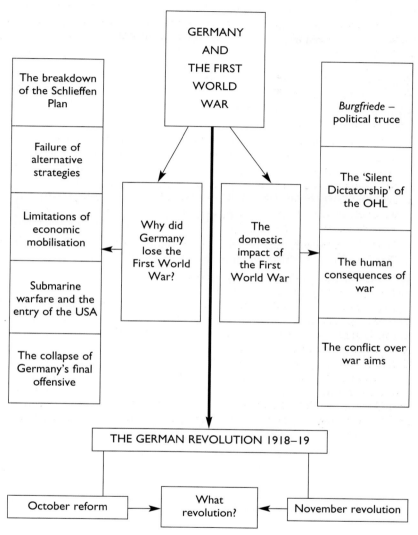

Working on Chapter 5

This chapter covers two important aspects of the First World War – the reasons Germany lost the war and the impact of the war on the German people. Therefore, you need to think out answers to two main questions:

1. Why did Germany lose the First World War?
2. What was the impact of the First World War on the German people?

Find as many different answers to these questions as you can. For each answer note down enough factual information to support the conclusion you have reached. When you have done this, decide on a rank order for the points you have made, starting with the most important.

Answering structured and interpretation questions on Chapter 5

Structured questions may be based on a relatively narrow topic or on a broader period of history. Here are examples of both.

1. **a)** What was the aim of the Schlieffen Plan? (*5 marks*)
    b) In what sense was the Plan flawed? (*5 marks*)
    c) To what extent was the Plan responsible for Britain's entry into the war? (*5 marks*)
    d) What were the long-term consequences of the failure of the Schlieffen Plan? (*5 marks*)
2. **a)** Explain the meaning of the terms *Burgfriede* and *Siegfriede*. (*2 × 2 = 4 marks*)
    b) For what reasons might the German decision to declare unrestricted submarine warfare in 1917 have been considered risky? (*6 marks*)
    c) To what extent had Hindenburg and Ludendorff become 'the silent dictators' of Germany by the end of the war? (*8 marks*)
    d) How succesful was the German leadership in regulating the country's war economy? Explain your answer fully. (*12 marks*)

Essay questions on Chapter 5

1. 'I see no parties any more. I see only Germans.' (Wilhelm II in a speech made at the outbreak of war in 1914.) How valid was the Kaiser's estimate of the solidarity of the German people during the course of the war?
2. 'The main reason for the defeat of Germany was the American intervention in the war. It's as simple as that.' (*Modern Germany* by Roger Morgan, 1966.) How valid is this assessment of the reasons for the defeat of Germany in the First World War?

6 The German Revolution, 1918–19

POINTS TO CONSIDER

This chapter considers the events that occurred in Germany during the last months of the war and the challenges faced by the new Republic during the first months of its existence. As you will see, these were difficult times for German politicians and the German people. Note the threat posed by those disenchanted by the war and its outcome who gave their support to extremist political groups. What options were open to Chancellor Ebert as he tried to cope with the situation? By the end of the chapter it should be possible to assess how close Germany was to revolution and estimate the Republic's chances of survival during the difficult times that lay ahead.

KEY DATES

1918	Sept	Ludendorff conceded that Germany was defeated
	Oct	Prince Max of Baden appointed Chancellor
	Nov	Grand Fleet mutinied at Kiel
		Bavaria proclaimed a socialist republic
		Kaiser fled to Holland. Ebert appointed Chancellor
		Germany proclaimed a republic. Armistice signed at Compiegne
	Dec	German Communist Party founded
1919	Jan	Start of Spartacist uprising in Berlin
	Feb	National Constituent Assembly met at Weimar
	June	Treaty of Versailles signed

1 October–November 1918 – The Political Situation

> **KEY ISSUE** To what extent did the constitutional changes represent a revolution from above?

a) *Dolchstosstheorie* – the 'Stab in the Back' theory

By late September 1918 the military defeat of Germany was a certainty and even Ludendorff recognised the fact. Faced with the prospect of an Allied invasion of German territory and the possibility of internal disturbances, Ludendorff sanctioned, with the Kaiser's consent, the conversion of Germany into a constitutional monarchy. Ludendorff's about-turn was mainly brought about by a two-fold desire. Firstly, he hoped to forestall a revolution amongst the people at large; secondly, he wanted to secure for Germany the best possible peace terms from the Allies. It was believed that the Allied leaders would be more likely to be sympathetic to a democratic regime in Berlin. Yet, even at this stage, Ludendorff had a third and far more cynical motive. There was already an apparent need to move responsibility for Germany's defeat away from the military and conservative establishment and instead put the blame on to appropriate scapegoats. Here lie the origins of the 'Stab in the Back' myth, which was later to play such a vital part in the history of the Weimar Republic. It was a theme soon taken up by others. In October, the Bavarian military attaché reported:

1 On the domestic political situation one often hears the opinion expressed that it is a good thing that the left-wing parties will have to incur the odium for peace. The storm of indignation of the people will fall on them … One hopes that then one can get back into the saddle
5 and continue to govern according to the old recipe.

b) Constitutional reforms

It was against this background that on 30 October 1918 Prince Max of Baden, a moderate conservative, became Chancellor. His government included representatives from the SPD and the Left Liberals. In the following month a series of constitutional reforms came into effect which made Germany into a parliamentary democracy. Wilhelm II gave up his powers over the army and the navy to the *Reichstag*; and the Chancellor and the government were made accountable to the *Reichstag* instead of to the Kaiser. At the same time, armistice negotiations with the Allies were opened.

Taken together, these changes have traditionally been portrayed as 'a revolution from above' since they were brought about by those in power and with influence and not forced 'from below' as a result of revolution. Structuralist historians, who regard the events of October 1918 as proving their theory that Germany had been controlled and manipulated by the elites, have not questioned such an interpretation. The German historian Hans Ulrich Wehler writes: 'The conservative bastions of the monarchy and the army were to be preserved as far as possible behind the facade of new arrangements intended to prevent the radical overthrow of the system and prove acceptable to the Allies'. However, more recently some historians have suggested that the steps taken by the Supreme Army Command coincided with increasing pressure from the *Reichstag* to bring about political change. The most telling evidence to support this is that a resolution passed on the same day as Ludendorff's recommendation for an armistice demanded 'the creation of a strong government supported by the confidence of a majority of the *Reichstag*'. Furthermore, Prince Max was appointed only after consultation with the majority parties in the *Reichstag*.

The idea that it was the *Reichstag* that brought about these changes certainly cannot be ignored but, on balance, it would be wrong to read too much into its actions. Over the years the *Reichstag* had shown no real inclination to seize the initiative. When opportunities such as The *Daily Telegraph* affair, the Zabern affair and the peace resolution had arisen, it had made no real attempt to press home its advantage. The same applied in 1918. The *Reichstag* suspended proceedings on 5 October and went into recess until 22 October when it adjourned again until 9 November. These were hardly the actions of an institution that wished to shape events decisively. It seems that the October reforms were imposed from above and the *Reichstag* was happy to go along with this. However, it would be an exaggeration to see these constitutional changes as representing a revolution. The forces that had dominated imperial Germany were still firmly in position at the end of the month. What pushed Germany, in such a short space of time, from political reform towards revolution was the widespread realisation that the war was lost. The shock of defeat, after years of hardship and optimistic propaganda, hardened popular opinion. By early November it was apparent that a constitutional monarchy, with Wilhelm II as Kaiser and a prince as Chancellor, would not ease what had become a revolutionary situation.

2 The Birth of the German Republic

> **KEY ISSUE** How close to a national revolution was Germany in November 1918?

a) The November Revolution

There can be little doubt that a genuinely revolutionary situation existed in Germany in early November 1918. What is more debatable is the nature and extent of the revolutionary feeling. What were the political alternatives facing Germany at this time? Why did the so-called November Revolution result in the creation of the Weimar Republic as opposed to any other system?

Prince Max's government began to lose control of the political situation as a result of a sailors' revolt at Kiel. This had been prompted by a real fear amongst sailors that their officers were planning a suicide attack on the British fleet in order to redeem the honour of the German navy. The news of the Kiel mutiny fanned the flames of discontent throughout Germany and by 8 November numerous workers' and soldiers' councils, similar to the soviets that had been set up by the Bolsheviks in Russia, had been established in the major cities. In Bavaria, the last of the House of Wittelsbach was deposed and an independent democratic socialist republic was proclaimed. Such a wave of popular discontent suggests that the October reforms had failed to impress, and that a revolutionary movement had developed whose

The left in German politics		
Social Democratic Party (SPD)	Independent Social Democratic Party (USPD)	The Spartacist League, later the German Communist Party (KPD)
The largest group in the *Reichstag*. A moderate socialist party, it drew its support from working and lower middle classes.	A splinter party that broke away from the SPD in 1917. It was more radical than the SPD and disapproved of that party's moderate line and was strongly anti-war.	Formed in 1918 by members of the Spartacist League, it represented the extreme left in German politics.

minimum demands were immediate peace and the abdication of Kaiser Wilhelm.

The revolutionary wave that swept Germany was not a united force. There were three strands to the revolutionary movement. The German Social Democratic Party, (the SPD), led by Friedrich Ebert and Philipp Scheidemann, represented moderate socialism intent on social reform. Above all, the party upheld democracy and it rejected totally anything that might have been likened to Soviet-style communism. An editorial in its newspaper on 24 December 1918 stated:

1 It was hunger that forced the Russian people under the yoke of militarism. Russia's workers went on strike, destroyed the economy through over-hasty socialisation, deprived themselves of the means of making a living through unrealisable demands, and sacrificed their free-
5 dom to militarism. Bolshevik militarism is the violent despotism of a clique...

Let the Russian example be a warning. Do we want another war? Do we want terror, the bloody reign of a caste? NO! We want no more bloodshed and no militarism. We want to achieve peace through work.
10 We want peace, in order not to degenerate into a militarism dictated by the unemployed, as in Russia. Bolshevik bums call the armed masses into the streets, and armed masses, bent on violence, are militarism personified. But we do not want militarism of the right or of the left.

Bolshevism, the lazy man's militarism, knows no freedom or equality.
15 It is vandalism and terror by a small group that arrogates power. So do not follow Spartacus, the German Bolsheviks, unless you want to ruin our economy and trade.

b) The Spartacists

On the extreme left stood the Spartacists, led by Polish-born Rosa Luxemburg, one of the few women to be prominent in German political history, and Karl Liebknecht, a former friend of Karl Marx. Encouraged by events in Russia, they believed that Germany should follow a similar road. They campaigned for a socialist republic, based on the people's power or the rule of the *proletariat*. Workers' and soldiers' councils would abolish the institutions of imperial Germany. To these ends they rejected the SDP's *bourgeois* compromises and took to the streets organising demonstrations, strikes, and eventually an armed uprising.

ROSA LUXEMBURG (1871–1919)

-Profile-

1870 born in Poland.
1905 took part in the troubles in Russia.
1914 imprisoned for the duration of the war.
1918 joined Liebknecht and founded the Spartacist League.
1919 murdered during the Spartacist uprising.

Rosa Luxemburg, or 'Red Rosa' as she became known, was born in Poland of Jewish origins. As a result of her revolutionary activities in Russia, she spent the war years in prison. Afterwards, she married a German in order to gain his nationality. In Germany, she was one of the founders of the Spartacist League and continued to champion the cause of armed revolution. In association with Karl Liebknecht, she called for a 'real revolution' that would sweep the capitalist system away. Luxemburg, who was severely handicapped and walked with a limp, endured continual pain. Taken into police custody during the Spartacist uprising in January 1919, she was murdered and her body thrown into a canal. Ironically she had been against the attempted coup. Later she was described as 'arguably one of the finest political theorists of the twentieth century'. Famously she said 'Freedom is always for the person who thinks differently'.

The Spartacist manifesto of 1918 stated:

1 The question today is not democracy or dictatorship. The question that
   history has put on the agenda reads: bourgeois democracy or socialist
   democracy. For the dictatorship of the proletariat is democracy in the
   socialist sense of the word. Dictatorship of the proletariat does not
5 mean bombs, putsches, riots and anarchy, as the agents of capitalist
   profits deliberately and falsely claim. Rather, it means using all instru-
   ments of political power to achieve socialism, to expropriate the capitalist class, through and in accordance with the will of the revolutionary
   majority of the *proletariat.*

Caught between the two extremes of the revolutionary movement was
the USPD. It demanded social and economic change as well as political reforms, fearing that otherwise democracy would not survive.
However, as a political movement it was far from united and internal
divisions and squabbles seriously curtailed its influence. The main disagreement was between those who sympathised with the creation of a
parliamentary democracy and those who advocated a much more
revolutionary democracy based on the workers' councils. The range
of differing aims and methods amongst the revolutionaries is in part
an explanation of why the events of November 1918 are so very confusing for the history student. However, it should be remembered
that many leading political figures at the time were trying to make
decisions in a society that was in a state of near collapse.

c) Ebert's coalition government

Prince Max would certainly have liked to preserve the monarchy, and
possibly even Wilhelm II himself. However, the Emperor's delusions
that he could carry on placed the Chancellor in a difficult position. In
the end, Prince Max became so worried that the revolutionary situation in Berlin might be getting out of hand that on 9 November he
announced the formation, under Ebert, of a new coalition government made up of the SPD and USPD. This government proclaimed
Germany a republic. It was only at this point that the Kaiser, advised
by leading generals, accepted the reality of the situation and went into
voluntary exile in Holland.

Ebert's main worry was that in this situation the extreme left would
gain the upper hand. He saw the growing number of workers' councils as similar to Russian-style soviets and feared that they might
threaten his policy of gradual change. He was determined to prevent
the country lapsing into civil war by maintaining law and order. He
also feared that the return of millions of troops after the armistice
agreement, which was eventually signed on 11 November, would
create enormous social and political problems. These were the main
concerns in the minds of Ebert and the SPD leadership in the months
that followed.

d) The Ebert–Groener agreement

On 10 November General Wilhelm Groener, Ludendorff's successor, telephoned Ebert. The Supreme Army Command agreed to support the government and to maintain law and order, in return for a promise from Ebert to resist Bolshevism and to preserve the authority of the officers. The Ebert–Groener agreement was followed a few days later by the Stinnes–Legien agreement between the employers and the trade unions. In return for a commitment not to interfere with private ownership and the free market, the unions were guaranteed full legal recognition, workers' committees and an eight-hour working day. These two agreements were severely criticised, particularly by the left wing, since they were regarded as compromises with the forces of conservatism. For Ebert and the SPD, however, they not only acted as guarantees of stability and peaceful transition, but also strengthened the government's hand against the extreme left.

By early 1919 it was clear that the SPD had become distanced from the USPD, its previous allies on the left. On 1 January 1919 the Spartacists formally founded the *Kommunistische Partei Deutschlands,* the KPD – German Communist Party. It refused to participate in the parliamentary elections, preferring instead to place its faith in the workers' councils. Meanwhile, the USPD members of Ebert's government had resigned over the shooting of some Spartacists by soldiers. As the SPD government became increasingly isolated, so it moved further to the right and grew dependent on the civil service and the army to maintain effective government. The reality of what was happening was revealed when, in January 1919, the Spartacists took part in an armed rising aimed at overthrowing the government. They had little chance of success. The government not only used army troops, but also 'irregular' military-style groups, *Freikorps.* The *Freikorps* were right-wing nationalist ex-soldiers who were only too willing to use force to suppress communist activity.

The Spartacist *coup* was easily defeated and afterwards Liebknecht and Luxemburg were brutally murdered whilst in police custody. This event set the tone for the next few months. The elections for the National Assembly duly took place, although the continuation of strikes and street disorders in Berlin meant that for reasons of security the Assembly's first meeting was switched to the town of Weimar. More serious disturbances in Bavaria in April resulted in a short-lived soviet-type republic being established there. The *Freikorps* brought both episodes under control, though in each case at the cost of several hundred lives. The infant republic had successfully survived the traumas of its birth.

For many years historians assumed that there had only ever been two possible options available to Germany at the end of the war, and that the people had to choose between a communist dictatorship or a parliamentary republic in the style of Weimar. In this way, Ebert was portrayed as a near heroic figure whose actions had saved Germany from Bolshevism. Following extensive research in the 1960s, this view has been revised. Close analysis of the workers' councils movement throughout Germany has shown that very few fell under the control of the extreme left. The vast majority were led by the SPD with USPD support and it was only after January 1919 that the USPD came to dominate. Thus, it is now generally recognised that the threat from the communists was grossly exaggerated. They may well have been vocal in putting forward their revolutionary creed, but their actual base of support was minimal. This evidence has, in turn, led to a reassessment of Ebert and the SPD leadership. Although their integrity and sincerity have not been questioned, it is claimed that their reading of the political situation was poor. Blinded by their fear of the left, they exaggerated the threat from that quarter and thereby compromised with the conservative forces of imperial Germany, when in actual fact there was no need, if only they had been prepared to assert authority. In that sense, they missed the opportunity to create a solidly based republic built on socialist and democratic principles.

3 Conclusion

By May 1919 a degree of stability had returned to Germany. The revolution had run its course and the Weimar Republic had been established. However, serious doubts remain about the nature and real extent of these revolutionary changes. Indeed, some historians argue that there was no real revolution at all.

Undoubtedly, there existed the possibility of revolutionary upheaval in Germany as the war came to an end. The effects of war and the shock of defeat shook the faith of large numbers of the people in the old order. The *Kaiserreich* could not survive and it did not. The Kaiser and the other princes were deposed and parliamentary democracy was introduced. These were important changes. However, in the end, the revolution did not go much further than the October reforms and was strictly limited in scope. Society was left almost untouched by these events for there was no attempt to reform the key institutions. The civil service, judiciary and army all remained essentially intact. Similarly, the power and influence of Germany's industrial and commercial leaders remained unchanged. Improved working conditions were introduced but there were no changes in the structure of big business and land ownership. The SPD leadership hoped that changes would follow constitutional reform but, with hindsight, it seems that the demands for more thoroughgoing social and economic changes made by the USPD might well have been the more likely policy to bring about the establishment of democracy. As it was, the divisions on the left played into the hands of the forces of conservatism on the right. As one historian has claimed – 'it is more accurate to talk of a potential revolution which ran away into the sand

Cheers Noske! The Young Revolution is Dead. (A satirical cartoon by George Grosz, 1919 shows the savagery of the *Freikorps*.)

rather than the genuine article'. Indeed, during the first half of 1919 the increasing dependency of the moderate left on the elites of the former *Kaiserreich* suggests that the forces of counter-revolution were once again beginning to assert a major influence in German politics.

Working on Chapter 6

This chapter was concerned with two important years in the immediate post-war history of Germany. Consider just how close the country might have been to falling victim of a Bolshevik-inspired revolution which, had it been successful, would have had a dramatic effect on events in Europe as a whole. What is suggested by the increase in violence in Germany and the agreement between Ebert and Groener? What did these suggest about what might happen in the future? The chapter has also considered the issue of how great was the threat to the Republic. Did the left-wing revolutionaries really constitute a threat to the life of the Republic? To what extent did the situation in Germany in 1919 mirror that of Russia in 1917?

Answering essay questions on Chapter 6

At AS and A2 levels, essay questions will require you to investigate the causes, effects and consequences of historical events and developments. Whilst accurate factual recall – remembering the historical detail – is obviously important, far greater importance is attached to you providing evidence of your ability to analyse, evaluate and develop an argument. Essay questions may introduce topics with such phrases as 'To what extent...', 'With what justification...', 'How significant was...', 'How valid is...' or simply 'Discuss'. As for format, the usual essay style is to divide your response into three sections – introduction (a brief outline of your approach to the topic), development (the main content of your answer that will include any factual detail, argument and analysis) and conclusion (your concluding comments). Before starting, some students like to get their thoughts together by preparing an outline or skeleton answer. This is a good idea but be careful that it is not too time consuming. In a good essay answer, it is necessary to make clear to the examiner that you have understood the question and identified the issues raised. You must make sure that you answer the question in full and direct your answer to the requirements of the question. You must also try to blend relevant narrative with analysis and discussion. Two major flaws that can lead to students failing to gain their expected grades are misreading the question and running out of time. Make sure you understand the exact nature of the question and plan your time allocation. Incomplete answers or answers written in haste in note form will lose a lot of marks – probably many more than you will have gained by spending more time on earlier questions.

Here are some essay-type questions based on the chapters you have covered so far:

1. To what extent did the legacy of Bismarck influence German politics after 1890?
2. 'Wilhelm II was totally in control and his personal rule complete.' How valid is this assessment of the German political scene in 1914?
3. Was German policy the main reason for the outbreak of a European war in 1914?
4. With what justification might it be claimed that the failure of the Schlieffen Plan in 1914 was the main reason why Germany failed to win the war?
5. How close was Germany to revolution in 1918–19? Explain your answer fully.

7 Weimar: The Years of Crisis, 1919–24

POINTS TO CONSIDER

During the period 1919–1933, the Weimar Republic passed through three distinct phases. Firstly there were years of crisis, then years of relative stability and finally years of renewed crisis which culminated in Adolf Hitler and the Nazis coming to power. In this chapter we are going to study the first phase when the Weimar Republic faced acute political and economic problems. You will need to consider the extent to which the political and economic problems were related and the degree of success that the various governments of the Weimar Republic achieved in coping with them. Remember that many of the problems faced by the Republic were consequences of losing the war and being forced to accept the terms of the treaty that followed. Make sure you identify the nature of the threats faced by the Republic and form your own opinion about how serious they were. Bear in mind too the on-going threat posed to the Republic by the extremist political parties of both the right and left.

KEY DATES

1919 Spartacist uprising in Berlin
National Constituent Assembly elected
Ebert first President of the Weimar Republic
Treaty of Versailles signed
1920 Kapp *putsch*. Hitler appointed leader of German Workers' Party
1921 Murder of Erzberger
1922 Murder of Rathenau
1923 Franco-Belgian occupation of the Ruhr
Period of hyper-inflation
Stresemann made Chancellor of Germany
Nazi 'Beer Hall' *putsch* in Munich
1924 Dawes Plan introduced
Increase in Nationalist and Communist representation in the *Reichstag*

1 The Political Situation in Post-War Germany

> **KEY ISSUE** What was the party structure during the Weimar Republic?

Despite the disturbances across Germany in the months after the collapse of the *Kaiserreich*, the new republic was able to hold its first elections for a National Assembly on 19 January 1919. Most political parties took the opportunity to re-form, but new names should not disguise the fact that there was considerable continuity in the structure of the party system (see the table below). In the end, the results represented a major success for the forces of parliamentary democracy. Over three-quarters of the electorate voted for the three parties committed to the new republic – the SPD, the DDP and the Centre – which then proceeded to form the first government, the so-called 'Weimar Coalition'. However, the creation of a broadly based democratic coalition did not result in a period of stability for the young republic. The years after 1919 were ones of almost continuous crisis and on several occasions the very survival of Weimar democracy seemed in doubt.

THE MAJOR POLITICAL PARTIES IN THE WEIMAR REPUBLIC

DDP Deutsche Demokratische Partei. German Democratic Party. Formed from the old DFP or Left Liberals, it attracted support from the professional middle classes. The party upheld a curious blend of liberal and nationalist ideas.

ZP Zentrumspartei. Centre Party. Initially, it tried to establish itself as the non-denominational Christian People's Party, but this was unsuccessful and it continued to be the voice of Catholicism. Its social composition was extremely broad, ranging from aristocratic landowners to Christian trade unionists. Not all sections of the party were wholly committed to the republic.

BVP Bayerische Volkspartei. Bavarian People's Party. A strong regional and Catholic party that left the ZP in 1919 because of the latter's support for centralised government.

DVP Deutsche Volkspartei. German People's Party. A new party founded by Gustav Stresemann who was excluded from the DDP during the First World War because he favoured waging war in order to make territorial gains. Conservative and monarchist, it was initially luke-warm towards the republic, but under Stresemann's influence it became a strong supporter of parliamentary democracy.

DNVP Deutschenationale Volkspartei. German National People's Party. A right-wing party formed from the old conservative parties and some of the racist, anti-Semitic groups such as the Pan-German League. Monarchist and anti-republican, it was closely tied to the interests of heavy industry and the landowners.

NSDAP Nationalsozialistische Partei Deutschlands. Nazi Party.

Extreme right-wing party formed in 1919. It was anti-republican, anti-Semitic and strongly nationalist.

SPD   Sozialdemokratische Partei Deutschlands. German Social Democratic Party. The moderate wing of the socialist movement, it was very much the party of the working class and the trade unions. It strongly supported parliamentary democracy and was opposed to the revolutionary demands of the more left-wing socialists.

USPD   Unabhängige Sozialdemokratische Partei Deutschlands. Independent German Social Democratic Party. The USPD broke away from the SPD in April 1917. It included many of the more revolutionary elements of German socialism and therefore sought radical social and political change. Some joined the KPD during 1919–20 whilst by 1922 most of the others had returned to the ranks of the SPD.

KPD   Kommunistische Partei Deutschlands. German Communist Party. Formed in December 1918 by the extreme left wing, e.g. Spartacists. Anti-republican in the sense that it opposed Weimar-style democracy and supported a revolutionary overthrow of society. Bolstered by the defection of many USPD members in 1920.

2 The Weimar Constitution

> **KEY ISSUE** What difficulties might the Weimar Constitution create for future governments?

a) The Constitution

THE PRESIDENT

Elected every seven years, he was a non-political figure responsible for nominating the Chancellor. He was supreme commander of the armed services. He had the power to summon and dissolve the *Reichstag* and, by Article 48 of the Constitution, had the right to rule by decree at a time of national emergency.

THE CHANCELLOR

Usually, though not always, the leader of the largest party in the *Reichstag*. In order to form a workable coalition government, he had to negotiate with the leaders of other political parties.

REICHSRAT

Made up of delegates nominated by the parliaments of the various states, the *Lander.* Acted as an advisory body and only had the power to delay legislation.

REICHSTAG

Elected every four years by proportional representation, its deputies formed the important law-making body of the German parliament.

b) The new Constitution – some considerations

In view of the fact that the Weimar Republic only lasted for 14 crisis-ridden years, it is hardly surprising that its written constitution has been the focus of considerable attention. Some historians have gone so far as to argue that in its clauses are to be found the real causes of the collapse of the Republic and the success of Hitler and National Socialists. Such claims are based on three aspects of the constitution. These are:

- the introduction of proportional representation (proportional representation allocates to each of the parties in an elected assembly a proportion of the seats depending on the number of votes it polled in the election);
- the relationship between the president and the *Reichstag* and, in particular, the emergency powers available to the president under Article 48;
- the fact that institutions of the *Kaiserreich* were allowed to continue.

The introduction of proportional representation became the focus of criticism after 1945 because it was argued that it encouraged the formation of new, small splinter parties. These, in turn, made it more difficult to form and to maintain governments and led to political instability. However, it is difficult to see how an alternative voting system based upon a British style of 'first past the post' could have made for a more effective parliamentary democracy. The main problem was the difficulty of creating coalitions and agreeing policies amongst the main parties. By comparison, the existence of the splinter parties would seem a relatively minor issue. There is also the view that, after 1929, proportional representation encouraged the emergence of political extremism. However, it now seems clear that the changes in the way people voted and the way they changed their allegiance from one party to another were just too dramatic to be kept in check. It may also have been the case that a 'first past the post' system would have actually helped the rise of Nazism and Communism.

The relationship created between the *Reichstag* and the president reflected the uncertainties felt by many of those drawing up the new constitution about the establishment of a democracy based upon the unrestricted rule of parliament. Fears of giving so much power to an elected parliament were not only strong on the right wing. They were also strong within liberal circles and this resulted in the creation of a presidency that was deliberately intended to limit the powers of the *Reichstag*. The president was to be directly elected by the people for seven years. He was to be the supreme commander of the armed forces and he alone convened and dissolved the *Reichstag*. He also appointed the chancellor and the Reich government. The powers of the president have often been seen as amounting to those of an *Ersatzkaiser*, a substitute emperor. When the power of the president is compared with the authority of the *Reichstag*, it seems that the attempt to prevent too much power being placed in the hands of one institution resulted in massive power being granted to another. As a result, there was uncertainty in constitutional matters from the start. Was the ultimate source of authority in the democratic republic vested in the representative assembly of the people, the *Reichstag*, or in the popularly elected head of state, the president?

c) Article 48

This situation was also made difficult by the powers conferred upon the president by Article 48. This Article provided the head of state with the authority to suspend civil rights in an emergency and to take whatever action was required to restore law and order by the issue of presidential decrees. The intention was to create the means by which government could continue to function in a crisis. However, the effect was to create what the historian Gordon Craig referred to as 'a constitutional anomaly' which could allow parliamentary government to be sidetracked by forces outside parliament acting on the orders of the President. Of course, such fears, which were actively expressed by some deputies in the constitutional debate of 1919, later assumed a particular importance during the crisis that eventually brought Hitler to power in 1933. However, it should be remembered that in the crisis of 1923 the presidential powers were used as intended and to good effect.

In a strange way, the Weimar constitution combined the continuity of old, traditional institutions with the introduction of a wide range of civil liberties. The civil service, the judiciary and the education system were all preserved in their old forms. In addition, the vast majority of bureaucrats, judges and professors many of whom were luke-warm or indeed actively hostile to the Republic, were confirmed in their positions. The result was that powerful conservative forces were able to exert great influence in the daily life of the Republic. This was at odds with the socialist intention of extending civil rights so that they were in line with the needs of a modern, democratic society. So it was that whilst the spirit of the constitution was demo-cratic and progressive, many of the institutions remained dedicated to the values of the *Kaiserreich*.

With hindsight, it is all too easy to highlight those parts of the Weimar constitution that contributed in some part to the ultimate collapse of the Republic. However, it should be remembered that, by providing a democratic framework, the new constitution was a great improvement upon the earlier undemocratic constitution of Bismarck. In July 1919, the new constitution was passed by the sub-stantial majority of 262 votes to 75 in the *Reichstag*. What the consti-tution could not control were the conditions and circumstances in which it had to operate. In this sense it is just unrealistic to imagine that any piece of paper could have made provision for all the possible consequences arising from Germany's problems and the difficulties caused by those opposed to it. Thirty years later in 1949, Theodor Heuss, the first President of the German Federal Republic created after the Second World War, said:

1 It is now fashionable ... to denigrate the Weimar Constitution. It is now customary to say that because Hitler's turn came and the provisions of the Weimar Constitution did not stop him, therefore this constitution was bad. The historical process does not work in quite so primitive a
5 manner.
The democracy of Weimar was so slow in getting off the ground and never got properly into gear because Germany never conquered democracy for herself. Democracy came to Germany – and this has become almost banal by now – in the wake of defeat. But because it was
10 not taken by storm it could not develop its own myth nor acquire its own know-how. Thus, it happened that the further evolution of democ-racy took place in an atmosphere of nationalist Romanticism and monarchical restoration and in the shadow of the wretched crime of the stab-in-the-back myth. These things were much more decisive in
15 governing the operation of the Weimar Constitution than the technical formulation of this or that constitutional paragraph, even if we may today consider some of them less than perfect.

3 The Treaty of Versailles

> **KEY ISSUE** Were the terms imposed on Germany at Versailles vindictive or just?

a) An agreed treaty or a '*diktat*'?

On 7 May 1919 the German delegation at the Paris Peace Conference was handed the draft copy of the proposed peace treaty. Two months later, after futile attempts to negotiate concessions and after the res-ignation of the Republic's first coalition government, Germany finally signed the Treaty of Versailles. No other political issue has produced such total agreement within Weimar Germany as in the rejection and condemnation of the Treaty of Versailles. The German case was based on a number of points. Firstly, the treaty was seen as a *Diktat*, a dictated settlement allowing for no negotiations and imposed under the threat of further Allied military action. Secondly, the treaty was considered to be very different from President Woodrow Wilson's Fourteen Points, upon which Germans believed the peace settlement was to be based. If self-determination, the right of people of the same race to decide their own form of government, was indeed the guiding principle of the Fourteen Points, Germany found it impossible to understand why Germans living in Austria, Danzig, Posen and West Prussia, Memel, Upper Silesia, the Sudetenland and the Saar were all excluded from the German state and placed under foreign rule. Likewise, the loss of German colonies that were committed to the care of the Allies as mandates was not in line with the fifth of Wilson's Fourteen Points which called for 'an impartial adjustment of all colonial claims'.

b) War guilt and reparations

Germany found it impossible to accept a 'war guilt' clause that was used as grounds for the payment of reparations. Most Germans had been convinced that the war of 1914 had been fought for defensive reasons and argued that in no way could Germany alone be held responsible for the outbreak of the war. Consequently, the Allied view that Germany was responsible and should be made to pay extensive reparations was seen as totally unreasonable, especially when the amount of money to be paid was not stated but was left to be decided by an Allied commission at a later date. From a German viewpoint this amounted to their being forced to sign a 'blank cheque'. Finally, Germany's treatment by the Allies was viewed as undignified and unworthy of a great power. For example, Germany was excluded from the League of Nations, an international organisation set up to settle disputes between nations peacefully, despite having to accept the rules of its covenant as part of the Treaty of Versailles. This simply hardened the views of those Germans who saw the League as a tool of the Allies rather than as a genuine international organisation. Likewise, the imposition of the disarmament clauses, which prohibited any kind of air force, reduced the German navy to virtual insignificance and limited the army to a mere 100,000 men, were seen as grossly unfair, particularly when the Allies had themselves made no commitments to disarm.

In the years 1919–45 such views were held by most Germans, while in Britain there was a growing sympathy for Germany. However, this was not the case in France, where the Treaty was generally condemned as being too lenient. It was only after the Second World War that a more balanced view of the Treaty of Versailles emerged. As a result, recent historians have tended to look upon the peacemakers of 1919 in a more sympathetic light and earlier German criticisms of the treaty have not been so readily accepted as they once were.

c) Versailles – some considerations

Of course, at the Paris peace conferences Allied statesmen were motivated by their desire to advance their own national interests, and the representatives of France and Britain were keen to achieve this at the expense of Germany. However, it is now recognised that the situation created by the war decided the terms of the treaty and not just anti-German feeling. The aims and objectives of the various Allies differed and achieving agreement was made more difficult by the complicated circumstances of the time. It should be remembered that the Paris peace settlement was not solely concerned with Germany but with Austria-Hungary, Bulgaria and Turkey as well. In addition, numerous other problems had to be dealt with. For example, Britain had national interests to look after in the Middle East as a result of the collapse of the Turkish Empire. At the same time the Allies were concerned by the possible threat of Soviet Russia and were motivated by a common desire to contain the Bolshevik menace.

In the end, the Treaty of Versailles was a compromise. It was not based on Wilson's Fourteen Points as most Germans thought it would be, but equally it was not nearly so severe as certain sections of Allied opinion had demanded. Georges Clemenceau, the French representative, was forced to give way over most of his country's more extreme demands, such as the creation of an independent Rhineland and the annexation of the Saar. Much contemporary German criticism was the result of nationalist propaganda and the shock of defeat. The application of self-determination was not nearly so unfair as many Germans believed. Alsace-Lorraine would have voted to return to France anyway and plebiscites were held in Schleswig, Silesia and parts of Prussia to decide their future. Danzig's status under the League was the result of Woodrow Wilson's promise to provide Poland with access to the sea whilst the eastern provinces of Posen and West Prussia were rather more mixed in ethnic make-up than Germans were prepared to admit. Finally, in comparison to the territorial terms imposed by the Germans on the Russians at Treaty of Brest–Litovsk in 1918, the Treaty of Versailles appears relatively moderate.

d) The significance of the Treaty of Versailles

However, the historical significance of the Treaty of Versailles goes well beyond the debate over its fairness. Even more important is the issue of its impact upon the Weimar Republic. Was Versailles a serious

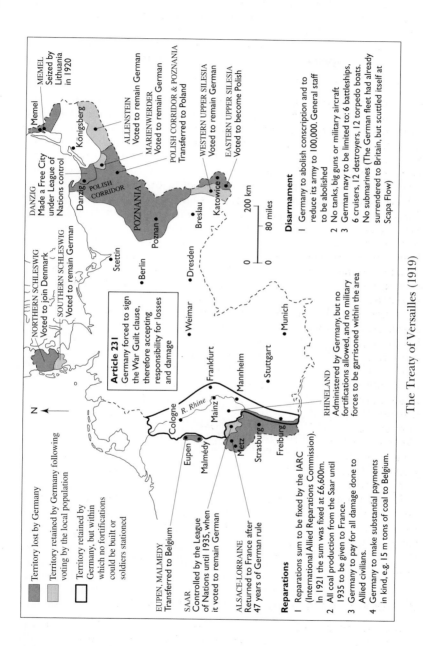

The Treaty of Versailles (1919)

Territory lost by Germany

Territory retained by Germany following voting by the local population

Territory retained by Germany, but within which no fortifications could be built or soldiers stationed

EUPEN, MALMEDY
Transferred to Belgium

SAAR
Controlled by the League of Nations until 1935, when it voted to remain German

ALSACE-LORRAINE
Returned to France after 47 years of German rule

Reparations

1 Reparations sum to be fixed by the IARC (International Allied Reparations Commission). In 1921 the sum was fixed at £6,600m.

2 All coal production from the Saar until 1935 to be given to France.

3 Germany to pay for all damage done to Allied civilians.

4 Germany to make substantial payments in kind, e.g. 15 m tons of coal to Belgium.

Article 231
Germany forced to sign the War Guilt clause, therefore accepting responsibility for losses and damage

NORTHERN SCHLESWIG
Voted to join Denmark

SOUTHERN SCHLESWIG
Voted to remain German

MEMEL
Seized by Lithuania in 1920

DANZIG
Made a Free City under League of Nations control

ALLENSTEIN
Voted to remain German

MARIENWERDER
Voted to remain German

POLISH CORRIDOR & POZNANIA
Transferred to Poland

WESTERN UPPER SILESIA
Voted to remain German

EASTERN UPPER SILESIA
Voted to become Polish

RHINELAND
Administered by Germany, but no fortifications allowed, and no military forces to be garrisoned within the area

Disarmament

1 Germany to abolish conscription and to reduce its army to 100,000. General staff to be abolished

2 No tanks, big guns or military aircraft

3 German navy to be limited to: 6 battleships, 6 cruisers, 12 destroyers, 12 torpedo boats. No submarines (The German fleet had already surrendered to Britain, but scuttled itself at Scapa Flow)

Memel
Königsberg
Danzig
POLISH CORRIDOR
POZNANIA
Poznan
Breslau
Katowice
Stettin
Berlin
Dresden
Weimar
Frankfurt
Mannheim
Stuttgart
Munich
Cologne
Mainz
Metz
Strasburg
Freiburg
Eupen
Malmédy
R. Rhine

N

0   80 miles
0   200 km

handicap to the establishment of long-term political stability in Germany? If so, how significant was it to the Republic's eventual collapse?

In terms of the political and economic limits imposed by Versailles, it is no longer possible to maintain that the treaty was excessively harsh. As will be seen in the course of the next two chapters, the Republic's economic problems cannot be blamed on the burden of reparations alone. In some respects, in 1919 Germany was in a relatively stronger position than in 1914. The great empires of Russia, Austria-Hungary and Turkey had gone, creating a power vacuum in central and eastern Europe that could not be filled by a weak and isolated USSR or by any other states. In such a situation, cautious diplomacy might have led to the establishment of German power and influence at the heart of Europe. In truth, the Treaty of Versailles should not be regarded as having placed limits on the Weimar Republic's successful development. From another viewpoint, the treaty might be considered more to blame since, in the minds of many Germans, it was regarded as the real cause of the country's problems. As a result, the Treaty of Versailles provided propaganda that those opposed to the Republic used to attack the Weimar system. Even for sympathetic democrats like Hugo Preuss, Versailles only served to disillusion many into thinking that the gains of the revolution were being undone. He wrote in 1923:

> 1 ...one must first weigh the tremendous obstacles which are being put in the path of the new constitution from abroad. The suspicious foreign countries have the least right of all to level such criticism at our internal development; for the most important cause of all those obstacles is the
> 5 illegal maltreatment of the national democracy by the victors over the Prussian Kaiserdom. If the latter was born out of the brilliance of victory, the German Republic was born out of its terrible defeat. This difference in origin cast from the first a dark shadow on the new political order, as far as national sentiment was concerned; but initially the belief
> 10 still predominated that the new order was necessary for the rebirth of Germany. That is why the democratic clauses of the Weimar constitution met with relatively little resistance, despite the unrivalled severity of the armistice terms. For everyone still expected a peace settlement in accordance with Wilson's 14 Points, which all the belligerent coun-
> 15 tries had bindingly accepted as the basis for the peace. This would have left the new Germany with the political and economic chance to survive and gradually pull itself up again, instead of turning it into the pariah among European nations by malevolently draining its national life-blood. The criminal madness of the Versailles Diktat was a shameless blow in
> 20 the face to such hopes based on international law and political common sense. The Reich constitution was born with this curse upon it. That it did not collapse immediately under the strain is striking proof of the intrinsic vitality of its basic principles; but its implementation and evolution were inevitably fatefully restricted and lamed thereby.

25   The victorious powers, and France especially, justify their policy of
endlessly beating down Germany with the argument that the weakness
of the Republic and the strength of its reactionary and nihilistic enemies
do not permit confidence to arise in the durability of the new order;
and yet it is precisely this policy which has done everything and left
30 nothing undone to weaken the German Republic and strengthen its
enemies by destroying the belief that Germany could resurrect itself on
the basis of the new constitution.

In this way the Treaty of Versailles contributed to the internal political and economic difficulties that occurred in Germany after 1919.

4 The Economic and Social Crisis, 1919–23

> **KEY ISSUE** To what extent was the hyperinflation that affected
> Germany during 1923–4 self-inflicted?

a) The great inflation – background

In its early months, not only was the young republic faced by the difficulties caused by the Treaty of Versailles and the creation of a new
constitution, but it was also faced the problems created by the economic legacy left by the *Kaiserreich* and the war. A lack of money for
investment, imports exceeding exports to produce a large trade
deficit and the difficulties of adjusting a war economy to the needs of
peace-time production were certainly made worse by the loss of
important industrial regions under the terms of the Treaty of
Versailles. However, the main cause of Germany's economic problems was the huge increase of the amount of money in circulation as
the government printed more and more in order to pay the interest
on its massive debts. This led to runaway inflation, a situation in which
the amount of money in circulation greatly exceeds the value of

German inflation, 1914–23		
		Marks to the pound
	1914	20
	1919	250
Early	1921	500
Late	1921	1,000
	1922	35,000
	1923	16,000,000,000,000

goods and services produced and which, in turn, causes prices to rise. Between 1913 and 1919 the national debt had risen from 5,000 million marks to 144,000 million marks. Over the same period, the value of the mark against the dollar had fallen by over 60 per cent and the prices of basic goods had increased between three- and four-fold.

By 1923, Germany's economy was caught in a spiral of runaway inflation, known as hyperinflation, in which figures and values became totally meaningless. It is one of those historical episodes where accounts of individual incidents give a good idea what the situation was like:

1   You went into a cafe and ordered a cup of coffee at the prices shown on the blackboard over the service hatch: an hour later, when you asked for the bill, it had gone up by a half or even doubled... Bartering became more and more widespread. Professional people including
5   lawyers accepted food in preference to cash fees. A haircut cost a couple of eggs, and craftsmen such as watchmakers displayed in their shop windows: 'Repairs carried out in exchange for food'. Once I was asked at the box-office of our local flea pit cinema if I could bring some coal as the price of two seats... A student I knew had sold his gallery
10   ticket at the State Opera for one dollar to an American; he could live on that money for a whole week. The most dramatic changes in Berlin's outward appearance were the masses of beggars in the streets... The hardcore of the street markets were the petty black marketeers... In the summer of that inflation year my grandmother found herself unable
15   to cope. So she asked one of her sons to sell her house. He did so for I don't know how many millions of marks. The old woman decided to keep the money under her mattress and buy food with it as the need arose – with the result that nothing was left except a pile of worthless paper when she died a few months later.

What were the real causes of Germany's inflation? What were the social and economic consequences and who gained and who lost from the episode?

b) The causes

For many of those living in Weimar Germany the 1923 inflation was beyond their understanding. Life became so desperate and so chaotic that simple explanations, focusing on the financial greed and corruption of the Jews or the adverse consequences of the Treaty of Versailles, seemed very convincing to many people. Moreover, the incredible experiences of 1923 itself blinded many to the fact that prices had started to rise as far back as 1914. Now it is clear that any explanation of German hyperinflation cannot be limited to a study of the year 1923 alone but must consider the inflationary spiral started by the onset of war in 1914. Germany had made no financial provision for a long-drawn-out war (see page 69) and, because of political difficulties, the imperial government decided against making increases in taxation. Instead, it had borrowed massive sums by selling war bonds. When, from 1916, this proved insufficient, it simply allowed the national debt to grow. So, at a time of almost full employment and high demand, the economy had remained committed to the supply of weapons of war rather than satisfying the requirements of consumers. Victory, of course, would have allowed the *Kaiserreich* to settle its debts by claiming reparations from the Allies, but defeat meant that the Weimar Republic had to cope with massive costs of the First World War. By 1919 Germany's finances were in what the historian Volker Berghahn described as 'an unholy mess' and the republican government faced major problems.

Narrowing the gap between government income and expenditure and thereby controlling inflation and stabilising the mark could only be achieved by increasing taxation and cutting government expenditure. In view of Germany's domestic situation neither of these options was particularly attractive, since both would alienate support for the Republic, depress the economy and increase unemployment. Consequently, from 1919 the Weimar Republic continued to pursue a policy of deficit financing. Deficit financing means planning to increase the nation's debt by reducing taxation in order to give the people more money to spend and so increase the demand for goods and thereby create work. The government believed that this would enable Germany to overcome the problems of demobilisation – a booming economy would ensure there were plenty of jobs for the returning soldiers and sailors – and also reduce the real value of the national debt. Unfortunately, an essential part of this policy was to allow inflation to continue.

The reparations issue should be seen as only a minor contributory factor to the inflation. It was certainly not a main cause. When the reparations sum was finally fixed by the Reparations Commission at £6,600 million (132 billion gold marks), it simply added to the future economic burden facing the Weimar government. Instead of tackling the basic economic problem of inflation, the government proceeded to print large quantities of marks and sell them to obtain the stronger currencies of other countries, particularly the American dollar, in order to pay their reparations. This was not a solution. It was merely a short-term measure that had disastrous consequences. The mark went into sharp decline and inflation climbed even higher.

In 1922, when Germany had already been allowed to postpone several instalments of her reparations payments, an unsuccessful attempt was made to solve the crisis on an international level by calling a conference at Genoa. When, in July 1922, the German government made another request for a 'holiday' from making reparations payments, the final stage of the country's economic crisis began. The French government, at this time led by Raymond Poincaré, suspected German intentions and was determined to secure what it saw as

France's rightful claims. Therefore, when in early 1923 the Reparations Commission declared Germany to be in default, French and Belgian troops occupied the Ruhr, the industrial heartland of Germany. The invasion did help to unite the German people in opposition to it but, economically, the result was to send the inflationary spiral out of control.

The government embarked on a policy of passive resistance. It urged workers to go on strike and, in return for the continued payment of their wages, to refuse to co-operate with the French. At the same time the government was unable to collect taxes from the Ruhr and the French prevented the delivery of coal to the rest of Germany, thus forcing the necessary stocks of fuel to be imported. In this situation, the government's finances fell into total disarray and the mark collapsed to meaningless levels. By autumn 1923 it cost more to print a bank note than the note was worth and the *Reichsbank* was forced to use newspaper presses to produce sufficient money. The German currency ceased to have any value and the German people became dependent on barter.

The fundamental cause of the German inflation is to be found in the mismanagement of Germany's finances from 1914 onwards, even though the inflationary spiral did not increase at a even rate and there were short periods, as in the spring of 1920 and the winter of 1920–21, when it did actually slacken. However, at no time was there a willingness by any of the various German governments to bring spending and borrowing back within reasonable limits. Until the end of 1918 the cost of waging war was the excuse but, in the immediate post-war period, the various difficulties facing the new government meant that high levels of debt were allowed to continue. The payment of reparations simply added to an already desperate situation, in which the government found it more convenient to print money than to tackle the basic problems facing the economy. By the end of 1922, even before the French occupation of the Ruhr, hyperinflation had set in. Thereafter, the government made no effort to deal with the situation, preferring instead to enjoy the glory brought by the popular decision to encourage passive resistance. It was only in September 1923 when the German economy was on the verge of complete collapse that a new coalition government under Gustav Stresemann found the will to introduce an economic policy aimed at controlling the amount of money in circulation.

c) Winners and losers

It has been claimed that the worst consequence of the inflation was the damage done to the German middle class. Stresemann himself said as much in 1927 and later on it was generally assumed that the reason a large proportion of the middle class voted for the Nazis was because of their economic sufferings in 1923. In the light of recent historical research, such assumptions have come to be questioned and a much more complex interpretation has emerged about the impact of the inflation on the whole of society, including the middle class. However, you should remember that the following discussion of the effects of the hyperinflation on whole classes cannot do justice to the range of factors, such as region, age and personal circumstances that affected individuals differently. The key to understanding who gained and who lost during the period of hyperinflation lies in considering each individual's income and the extent of their indebtedness. Clearly, this could have been linked to class differences but it was not always necessarily so. So what did this mean in practice? It meant that the real winners were those sections of the community who were able to pay off their debts, mortgages and loans with inflated and worthless money. This obviously worked to the advantage of such groups as businessmen, landowners and homeowners, which must obviously have included some members of the middle class. Those who recognised the situation for what it was made massive gains by buying up more property from the gullible and desperate. Some businessmen were able to take advantage of the low interest rates and large profits and made sufficient money to create large industrial enterprises. Amongst these, one of the most notorious examples was Hugo Stinnes who, by the end of 1923, controlled twenty per cent of German industry. At the other extreme were those with savings and, especially, those millions who had bought war bonds who now found that their money had simply been invested or loaned for nothing. Some idea of the impact of the inflation can be gleaned from Erich Maria Remarque's novel *Der Schwarze Obelisk*, The Black Obelisk, in which a widow explains the suicide of her husband:

1   It was because of the money. It was in a guaranteed five-year deposit in the bank, and he couldn't touch it. It was the dowry for my daughter from my first marriage. He was the trustee. When he was allowed to withdraw it two weeks ago, it wasn't worth anything any more, and the
5   bridegroom broke off the engagement... My daughter just cried. He couldn't stand that. He thought it was his fault.

In a similar situation were those who were living on fixed incomes or pensions, or who received welfare support, such as students, the retired and the sick. Most grants and pensions gradually lost value since increases did not keep up with the pace of inflation.

Between the extremes of those who gained greatly and those who lost dramatically was the mass of the German population. In the countryside farmers coped reasonably well since food remained in demand and they were less dependent on money for the provision of the necessities of life. Shopkeepers and craftsmen also seem to have done good business, especially if they were prepared to exploit the black market. The impact on employees dependent on wages and salaries is the most difficult to interpret. The belief that workers' standard of living continued to decline after 1918 is now generally questioned and it seems that until 1922 the real value of wages continued to increase. It was only in the chaos of 1923, when the trade unions were unable to negotiate wage settlements for their members that could keep pace with the rate of inflation, that a decline took place. Moreover, for the workers there was the added security provided by the relatively low levels of unemployment. As for salaried officials, office workers and public employees, here too, the traditional picture of continuous loss of income has been shown to be inaccurate. According to the German historian CL Holtfrerich, the low point in real terms was actually in early 1920 and in 1921–2 real gains were made that were only partially lost in the events of 1923.

The material impact of the hyperinflation has recently been the subject of considerable historical research in Germany and, as a result, many previous conclusions have been revised. As a result of this research, our understanding of this period has been greatly increased. It now seems that there is little to be gained from making generalised lists of winners and losers amongst the social groups, for the reality was far more confused than was previously thought. Two people from the same social class could be affected in very different ways depending on their individual circumstances. In particular, levels of debt and amounts of savings were crucial to a person's material fortune or misfortune. Therefore, it seems that the most meaningful general conclusion that can be reached is that those with large debts benefited from the hyperinflation while those with large cash savings suffered greatly.

d) Was this period of inflation a total disaster for the German people?

Traditionally, the German inflation has been portrayed as an economic catastrophe with damaging consequences that paved the way later on for the collapse of the Weimar Republic and the rise of Hitler's National Socialists. However, in the 1980s a number of economic historians began to interpret the event differently. Holtfrerich maintains that in the years up to the end of 1922 Weimar's economic policy amounted to a 'rational strategy ... in the national interest'. His view is that, by continuing the policy of deficit financing, the Weimar Republic was able to maintain economic growth and increase production in a way that compared very favourably with other European economies. Most of these went into post-war recession in 1920–1. For example, whereas Britain had an unemployment rate of nearly 17 per cent in 1921, Germany had nearly full employment with only 1.8 per cent unemployed and rising wage levels. The high level of economic activity at this time also attracted foreign investment and large sums, especially from the USA, poured into

Germany. Finally, Holtfrerich claims that the policy was not only beneficial, but was in fact also the only way to ensure the survival of the
Weimar Republic. He argues that, in the early years, any policy that
required cutting back would have had the most terrible economic
and social consequences that probably would have destroyed the new
German democracy.

However, some find it difficult to accept Holtfrerich's view. He has
been criticised for drawing a line between the years up to 1922, a time
of what might be termed 'good inflation' and the hyperinflation of
1923 with all its accompanying problems. This seems a rather doubtful way of looking at developments bearing in mind the long-term
build up to the great inflation and the nature of its causes. It also
tends to separate the inflation from the drastic measures that were
eventually required to solve it. His argument is very much that of an
economic historian and is based largely on a study of economic and
financial factors. Consequently, his interpretation tends to pay less
regard to other important considerations. Above all, it has tended to
underestimate the disastrous effects of the inflation on certain sections of German society. In February 1923 the health minister deliv-
ered a speech to the *Reichstag*:

1 Unfortunately, this picture of accelerating and shocking decline in health
   conditions applies to the whole Reich. In the rural areas where many
   self-sufficient farmers are able to feed themselves and the difficulties
   resulting from a great density of population do not exist, conditions
5 seem to be better. But in the towns and in the districts with an industrial mass population, there has been a decided deterioration. Especially
   hard-hit are the middle-class, those living on small annuities, the widows
   and the pensioners, who with their modest incomes can no longer
   afford the most basic necessities at present day prices...
10   It is understandable that under such unhygienic circumstances, health
   levels are deteriorating ever more seriously. While the figures for the
   Reich as a whole are not yet available, we do have a preliminary mortality rate for towns with 100,000 or more inhabitants. After having
   fallen in 1920–1, it has climbed again for the year 1921–2, rising from
15 12.6 to 13.4 per thousand inhabitants... oedema (an unpleasant medical
   condition when occurs when water accumulates in parts of the body) is
   reappearing, this so-called war dropsy, which is a consequence of a bad
   and overly watery diet. There are increases in stomach disorders and
   food poisoning, which are the result of eating spoiled foods. There are
20 complaints of the appearance of scurvy, which is a consequence of an
   unbalanced and improper diet. From various parts of the Reich, reports
   are coming in about an increase in suicides... More and more often one
   finds 'old age' and 'weakness' listed in the official records as the cause
   of death; these are equivalent to death through hunger.

Even more awful were the effects on human behaviour. Profiteering,
crime and prostitution all increased at this time. It has often been

suggested that such behavioural problems contributed to people's lack of faith in the republican system. Such a connection is difficult to prove since it is not easy to assess the importance of morality and religious beliefs on past societies. However, it would be foolish to dismiss out of hand the possible effects upon German society of the decline in its traditional set of values. At the very least, the loss of some old values must have increased tensions. Perhaps, even more significantly, when yet another crisis developed at the end of the decade, the people's confidence in the ability of Weimar to maintain social stability was eventually lost. In that sense the inflation of 1923 was not the reason for the Weimar Republic's decline, but it caused psychological damage that continued to affect the Republic in future years.

5 The Political Crisis

> **KEY ISSUE** In what sense was the survival of the Weimar Republic during the period 1919–24 'almost a miracle'?

However much emphasis one wishes to place on the economic crisis facing Weimar Germany, it still remains true that, from the start, there were underlying problems in the political system which went far deeper than the criticisms made of the new constitution. In spite of the success of parties sympathetic to the Republic in the *Reichstag* elections of January 1919, such problems were to be found in the very nature of the Weimar political system. The Republic was faced by opposition from both the extreme left and extreme right, whilst its democratic supporters struggled with the problem of creating and maintaining workable government coalitions. During the years 1919–24, the effect of these political problems, worsened by the economic conditions and an uneasy relationship with neighbouring France, created an atmosphere of continuous crisis that reached its peak in 1923. Indeed, one historian goes as far as to claim that Weimar's very survival at this time should be viewed as 'almost a miracle'.

a) Left-wing opposition

After the revolution of 1918–19 the left-wing parties (see pages 101–2) remained in a state of confusion. The moderate socialists of the SPD were committed to parliamentary democracy; the Communists of the KPD, taking their lead from Bolshevik Russia, pressed for a proletarian revolution, whilst between them, the USPD pressed for the creation of a socialist society within a democratic framework. This situation became clearer when, in 1920, the USPD disbanded. This resulted in its members switching to either the KPD or the SPD. Major differences existed between these two parties. Why did the extreme left so strongly oppose the Weimar Republic? How serious was their opposition to the republic's future stability?

The KPD viewed the establishment of parliamentary democracy as no more than a 'bourgeois compromise'. It wanted the revolution to proceed on Marxist-Leninist lines with the creation of a one-party communist state and the major restructuring of Germany both socially and economically. Its opposition to the Weimar Republic was nothing less than a wholesale rejection of the system. It was not prepared to be part of the opposition and work within the parliamentary system to bring about its desired changes. The differences between the moderate and extreme left was so basic that there was no chance of political co-operation between them, let alone a coming together into one socialist movement. The extreme left was totally committed to a very different vision of German politics and society whereas the moderate left was one of the pillars of Weimar democracy.

Looking back, it is clear that the extreme left posed much less of a threat to Weimar than was believed at the time. Its support at 10–15 per cent of the electorate and its revolutionary actions, like the creation of a short-lived soviet republic in Bavaria in April 1919 and an attempted armed uprising in Saxony in March 1921, gave the impression of a Bolshevik inspired 'Red Threat'. As a result of propaganda, many of the extreme right began to have exaggerated fears about the possibility of impending revolution. In particular, it forced the parliamentary left and other democrats into depending on the forces of reaction to maintain the nation's security. However, the reality was not nearly so threatening. Even during the chaos and uncertainty of 1923, the activities of the extreme left were limited to several isolated incidents. It proved incapable of mounting a unified attack on Weimar democracy. Weakened by divisions and uncertainty, it was unsure what tactics it should employ. The repression it suffered at the hands of the *Freikorps* (see page 94) also removed some of its ablest and most spirited leaders. The result was that it was never able to gain more than about one-third of the support from the working class. In the end, the extreme left was just not powerful enough to lead a revolution against the Weimar Republic. However, its opposition, together with that the extreme right, created problems that adversely affected the Republic from the start.

b) Right-wing opposition

Opposition from the extreme right was very different both in its form and in its extent to that of the extreme left. On the right wing there was to be found a very mixed collection of opponents to the Republic and their resistance found expression in different ways. The threat from the extreme right must be regarded from several viewpoints. What did it stand for? Who or what was the extreme right? Did it pose a more serious threat to Weimar democracy than the extreme left?

The extreme right was united by its total rejection of the Weimar system and its principles. It sought to destroy the democratic constitution and to establish a nationalist-style dictatorship. It was this conservative-nationalist opposition that first encouraged belief in the 'stab in the back' myth. The war, it was argued, had been lost not because of any military defeat suffered by the army, but as a result of the betrayal of unpatriotic forces within Germany. These unpatriotic forces were said to include pacifists, socialists, democrats and Jews. Right-wing politicians found a whole range of scapegoats to take the blame for German acceptance of the armistice. Worse still, these 'November Criminals', as they were called, had been prepared to overthrow the monarchy and establish a republic. Then, to add insult to injury, they had accepted the 'shameful peace' of Versailles. The extreme right accepted such interpretations, distorted as they were, of the events of 1918–19. They not only served to remove any responsibility of the *Kaiserreich*, but also acted as a powerful stick with which to beat the new leaders of Weimar Germany.

The extreme right appeared in various forms. It included a number of political parties and was also the driving force behind the activities of various paramilitary organisations. Organisations such as the *Stahlhelm* and the *Sturmabteilung* were prepared to use violence when it suited. The German National People's Party, the DNVP, was a coalition of nationalist-minded old imperial conservative parties and included such groups as the Fatherland Party and the Pan-German League. From the very start, it contained extremist and racist elements. Although it was still the party of landowners and industrialists, it had a broad appeal amongst the middle classes and was able to poll 15.1 per cent in the 1920 election. Although the DNVP remained the dominant force on the extreme right until the depression set in at the end of the decade, there were also other fringe parties. The emergence of *völkisch* nationalism was clearly apparent before 1914, but the effects of the war and its aftermath led it to attract many on the right. Bavaria became a haven for such groups, since the state government was sufficiently reactionary to tolerate them. One such group was the German Workers' Party, originally founded by Anton Drexler. Adolf Hitler joined the party in 1919 and within two years had become its leader. However, during the years 1919–24, regional and policy differences divided such groups and attempts to unify the nationalist right ended in failure. It was not until the mid-1920s, when Hitler began to bring the different groups together under the leadership of the NSDAP, that a powerful political force was created.

In the early years of the Weimar Republic, the bullet rather than the ballot-box was the more active amongst nationalist extremists. Units of the *Freikorps* that flourished in the post-war environment attracted the more brutal and ugly elements of German militarism. Although they were occasionally employed by the government to suppress the threat from the extreme left, the *Freikorps* was anti-republican and committed to the restoration of authoritarian rule. They showed many of the worst features and blind prejudices of the extreme right and were prepared to use acts of violence and murder to intimidate others.

The *Freikorps* were almost certainly behind the gang called 'Organisation Consul' which assassinated the two key republican politicians, Matthias Erzberger and Walther Rathenau. They also played a central role in the first attempt by the right wing to seize power from the constitutional government in the Kapp-Lüttwitz *Putsch* of 1920.

In early 1920, the need to reduce the size of the German army according to the terms of the Versailles Treaty created considerable unease within the ranks of the *Freikorps*. When it was proposed to disband the Baltikum Brigade and a brigade commanded by Hermann Ehrhardt that had earlier been involved in brutally crushing the Spartacist uprising (see page 92), Kapp and Lüttwitz decided to exploit the situation and to march on Berlin. Unopposed, they entered the capital and installed a new government which issued the following proclamation:

WOLFGANG KAPP (1868–1922)

-Profile-

1857   born in New York
1870   returned to Germany with his family
1917   founded the right-wing German Fatherland Party
1919   elected to the *Reichstag*
1920   became involved with the *Freikorps* and was the leader of an attempted coup in Berlin
1922   died whilst awaiting trial

Wolfgang Kapp's father had been involved in revolutionary activity in Germany in 1848. This made it necessary for him to emigrate to the United States the following year. After returning to Germany in 1870, young Wolfgang studied law and spent some years managing an estate in East Prussia before being employed by the Prussian ministry of agriculture. He developed extreme right-wing views and was one of the founders of the German Fatherland Party. After the war, he was elected to the *Reichstag* and campaigned for the restoration of Kaiser Wilhelm II. In 1920, together with General von Lüttwitz, he led a group of *Freikorps* in an attempt to take control of Berlin and set up a new government. His attempted coup was a fiasco. Kapp has been described as 'a neurotic with delusions' or simply a 'crank'. Interestingly, some of the men involved in his *putsch* had swastika symbols on their helmets.

1   The *Reich* and the nation are in grave danger. With terrible speed we
are approaching the complete collapse of the State and of law and
order. The people are only dimly aware of the approaching disaster.
Prices are rising unchecked. Hardship is growing. Starvation threatens.
5   Corruption, usury, nepotism and crime are cheekily raising their heads.
The government, lacking in authority, impotent and in league with corruption is incapable of overcoming the danger. Away with a government
in which Erzberger is the leading light!...
     What principles should be our guide? Not reaction, but a free devel-
10   opment of the German State, restoration of order and the sanctity of
the law. Duty and conscience must reign again in the German land.
German honour and honesty must be restored ... The hour of the salvation of Germany is at hand and must be used; therefore there is no
other way but a government of action. What are the tasks facing the
15   new government?...
     The government will ruthlessly suppress strikes and sabotage.
Everyone should go peacefully about his work. Everyone willing to work
is assured of our firm protection: striking is treason to the nation, the
Fatherland and the future. The government will... not be a one-sided
20   capitalist one. It will rather save German workers from the hard fate of
slavery to international big business and hopes by such measures to put
an end to the hostility of the working classes to the State... We shall
govern not according to theories but according to the practical needs
of the State and the nation as a whole. In the best German tradition the
25   State must stand above the conflict of classes and parties. It is the objec-
tive arbiter in the present conflict between capital and labour. We
reject the granting of class-advantage to the Right or the Left. We
recognise only German citizens. Everyone must do his duty! The first
duty of every man is to work. Germany must be a moral working com-
30   munity!

c) The significance of the Kapp *putsch*

Significantly, the army did not provide any resistance to this *putsch*. In
spite of requests from Ebert and the Chancellor to put down the
rebellious forces, the army was not prepared to become involved with
either side. Although it did not join those involved in the *putsch,* it
failed to support the country's legitimate government. General von
Seeckt, the senior officer in the Defence Ministry, spoke for many col-
leagues when he declared:

> Troops do not fire on troops. So, you perhaps intend, Herr Minister,
> that a battle be fought before the Brandenburger Tor between troops
> that have fought side by side against a common enemy? When
> *Reichswehr* fires on *Reichswehr* all comradeship within the officers' corps
> will have vanished.

The army's decision to put its own interests before its obligation to defend the government forced the latter to flee the capital and move to Stuttgart. However, the *putsch* collapsed. Before leaving Berlin, the SPD members of the government had called for a general strike, which soon paralysed the capital and quickly spread to the rest of the country. After four days, it was clear that Kapp and his government exerted no real authority and they fled the city. At first sight the collapse of the Kapp *Putsch* could be viewed as a major success for the republic since it had retained the backing of popular opinion and effectively withstood a major threat from the extreme right. However, what is significant is that the Kapp *Putsch* had taken place at all! In this sense, the Kapp *Putsch* highlights all too clearly the weakness of the Weimar Republic. The army's behaviour at the time of the *putsch* was typical of their right-wing attitudes and their lack of sympathy for the Republic. During the months after the coup, the government failed to confront this problem.

The army leadership had revealed its doubtful reliability. Yet, amazingly, Seeckt was appointed Chief of the Army Command at the end of that very month. He was appointed because he enjoyed the confidence of his fellow officers and ignored the fact that his attitude to the Republic was at best lukewarm. Under Seeckt's influence, the army was remodelled and its status redefined. It now held a privileged position that placed it beyond direct government control. Many within its ranks believed that the army served some higher purpose to the nation as a whole and therefore it had the right to intervene as it saw fit without regard to its obligations to the Republic.

The judiciary also continued with its old political values that had not changed since imperial times. It questioned the legal rights of the new republic and reached some dubious and obviously biased decisions. Those involved in the *putsch* of 1920 were not charged with any crime. Kapp died awaiting trial whilst Lüttwitz was granted early

The White General by G. Gross

retirement. Even those who were brought to trial were only sentenced to five years' imprisonment! Such treatment was commonplace. After the attempted Nazi *putsch* in Munich in 1923, Hitler was sentenced to a mere five years, but was released after less than 12 months, whilst Ludendorff was acquitted altogether. In contrast, leaders of left-wing uprisings faced lengthy prison sentences and sometimes even the death penalty. There is no doubt that the judiciary was biased in favour of the extreme right and its judgements served to weaken the Republic and encourage right-wing opposition. Much the same could also be said for other key institutions such as the civil service and the educational establishment.

The extent of the opposition from the extreme right to the Weimar Republic was not always appreciated. It ranged from indifference to brutal violence. However, because of the threat from the extreme left, the republican regime came to rely on the forces of reaction and this was particularly true in the spheres of justice and law and order. In many respects it was this persistence of the old attitudes and the lack of support for democracy in the major national institutions which represented the greatest long-term threat to the Republic. The violent forces of counter-revolution, as shown by the *putsches* of Kapp and Hitler, were at this time too weak and disorganised to seize power. It was a lesson Hitler came to appreciate as he languished in prison during 1924.

6 Stresemann and the 'Miracle of the Rentenmark'

> **KEY ISSUE** Did acceptance of the Dawes Plan in 1924 set Germany on the road to economic recovery?

a) The appointment of Stresemann as Chancellor

In 1923, the crisis facing the Weimar Republic came to a head. French and Belgian troops occupied the Ruhr and with no effective means to oppose them the German government resorted to the policy of 'passive resistance' (see page 113). Meanwhile, the German currency collapsed and hyperinflation set in. As a result, various political disturbances took place across the country ending in an attempted Communist uprising in Saxony and the failed Hitler *putsch* in Bavaria. The Republic was very close to collapse. Yet, only a few months later a semblance of calm and normality had returned. The historian Peukert's telling comment that 1923 shows 'there are no entirely hopeless situations in history' not only illustrates the Weimar Republic's remarkable survival but also the difficulty for historians in explaining it. It is important to recognise that decisive political action was taken in the second half of 1923 to face the crisis and that the results were beneficial. Up until the end of 1922, things had just been allowed to slide, but the appointment of Gustav Stresemann as Chancellor in August 1923 witnessed the emergence of a politician who was actually prepared to make difficult decisions in an attempt to resolve Germany's economic plight and the weakness of her international position.

b) Stresemann's achievements

Stresemann called off passive resistance in the Ruhr and promised to resume the payment of reparations. He also sharply reduced government expenditure and so cut the deficit. He also introduced a new German currency, the *Rentenmark*. The result was to halt the hyperinflation, establish a stable currency, and make possible an international conference to consider Germany's economic plight. The 'miracle of the Rentenmark' and Stresemann's conciliatory policy gained Germany some sympathy from the Allies, and the Dawes Committee was established to examine Germany's financial position. Its report, the Dawes Plan published in April 1924, did not reduce the overall reparation bill, but for the first five years it fixed the payments in accordance with Germany's ability to pay. It also made arrangements for Germany to receive a large international loan. The acceptance of the Dawes Plan by both Germany and the Allies can be seen to mark the beginning of a new era both in international relations and in Germany's domestic condition.

Although Stresemann's resolute action in tackling the problems might help to explain why the years of crisis came to an end, on its own it does not help us to understand why the Weimar Republic was able to come through the years of crisis. The Republic's survival in 1923 was in marked contrast to its collapse ten years later. Why was this? Why did the Republic not collapse during the crisis-ridden months before Stresemann's emergence on the political scene?

It could be argued, for example, that popular resentment was directed more towards the French and the Allies than towards the Weimar Republic itself. It has also been suggested that, despite the effects of inflation, workers did not suffer to the same extent as they did at the time when there was long-term mass unemployment. Similarly, employers tended to show less hostility to the Republic in its early years than they did in the early 1930s at the start of the depression. Of course, some businessmen did very well out of the inflation. If these assumptions about attitudes towards the Republic are correct, then it seems that, although there was distress and disillusionment in 1923, hostility to the Weimar Republic had not yet reached the level it was to do later. Moreover, in 1923 there was no obvious political alternative to Weimar. The extreme left had not really recovered from its divisions and suppression in the years 1918–21 and in its isolated position it did not enjoy enough support to overthrow Weimar. The extreme right too was not yet strong enough. It was also divided and had no clear plans. The failure of the Kapp *Putsch* served as a clear warning of the dangers of taking hasty action and was possibly the reason why the army took no action in 1923. As we have seen, the Weimar Republic survived its post-war years of crisis. It is worth remembering that during this period the governments of other countries did not fare so well. Italy, a liberal democracy since 1870, and Hungary were already moving towards dictatorship and Poland soon followed. Up to 1923, the Republic had weathered the storm. Was this a sign of growing political strength and stability? If so, perhaps it could now begin to build on its achievements as it moved into the calmer waters of the mid-1920s.

Working on Chapter 7

In studying this chapter you will have come across several topics which remain areas of historical disagreement or where arguments have proved indecisive. This alone is indicative of the complexities of the years 1919–24. There is a great deal for you to consider. Firstly, there is the constitution of the Weimar Republic. To what extent might it be called democratic and what were its inherent weaknesses? Next you need to decide whether the Treaty of Versailles treated Germany fairly. Before you reach a conclusion bear in mind Germany's treatment of Russia by the Treaty of Brest–Litovsk when, as it were, the boot was on the other foot. The economic crisis of 1923 is another issue that needs to be considered from different viewpoints. Was it the outcome of Germany's struggle to pay her reparations or was it self-inflicted and the result of reckless economic policies? Or was there, perhaps, no such straightforward explanation? When considering the political crises caused by the activities of extremist political parties on both the left and right, give some thought to whether they ever really presented a threat to the future of the Weimar Republic? Finally, the chapter considers the reasons for the survival of the Republic. Think carefully about the nature of the solutions that were found to bring the economic and political crises to an end. Were they long-term or were the problems likely to reoccur again in the future when circumstances changed?

Summary Diagram
Weimar: The Years of Crisis, 1919–24

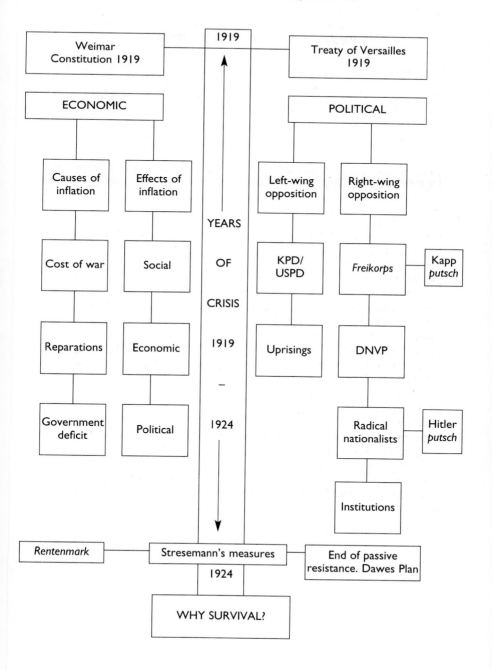

Source-based questions on Chapter 7

1 The years 1920–24 are still known as 'the period of inflation' in Germany. At the end of the war the mark was worth about half as much as in 1914... But in November 1923, a gold mark was worth one billion paper marks. This is how it appeared in figures: 1,000,000,000,000. The
5 demand for treasury notes was so great that the *Reichsbank* was unable to issue enough. In addition there were several private presses printing bank notes. Many local councils and industrial firms took to printing their own emergency notes to meet their expenses. During the whole of the period, neither the *Reichsbank* nor the government made any
10 effort to establish a stable currency. The board of the Reichsbank said that it was useless to stabilise the mark as it was uncertain how much Germany would be able to pay in reparations. Political unrest developed to a point where the stabilisation of money became a vital necessity if the country were not to collapse. Bank notes were sent in gigantic
15 bundles by lorry and railway wagon to the cities and provinces. In order to produce one currency note more time was required by paper makers, engineers, printers, lithographers, colour experts etc. than was represented by the value of the note.

(From My First Seventy-Six Years by Hjalmar Schacht, 1955.)

1. a) What is meant by 'a period of inflation'? (*2 marks*)
   b) Why, according to the source, i) did the *Reichsbank* feel that it was useless to try to stabilise the currency? ii) did it become vital for the government to stabilise the currency? (*2 × 4 = 8 marks*)
   c) How valuable is the source to an historian studying the causes of the German inflation? (*8 marks*)
   d) Use the source and your own knowledge to explain the effects of the inflation on the German people. (*12 marks*)

Essay questions on Chapter 7

1. With what justification might it be claimed that the problems that faced the Weimar Republic in the early 1920s were more economic than political?
2. 'It was little short of a miracle that, against all the odds, the Weimar Republic managed to survive 1923.' How valid is this judgement?

Weimar: Years of Relative Stability, 1924–29

8

POINTS TO CONSIDER

It is generally held that after the turmoil of the early 1920s, the period 1924–9 in German history was a period of gradual economic recovery and an advance towards political stability. In this chapter, we will consider the accuracy of this picture. We begin by studying the reasons for German economic recovery and consider if it was built on sound foundations. As part of this, we need to consider the contrasting views of the problems facing the German economy held by two German historians, Borchardt and Holtfrerich. We will then examine the extent to which the Weimar Republic had been able to achieve political stability. Remember that the latter part of this period witnessed some restoration of Nazi fortunes. Finally, we look at developments in German foreign policy and pay particular attention to the achievements of Gustav Stresemann.

KEY DATES

1924 The Dawes Plan
1925 Hindenburg elected President
Locarno Conference
1928 Müller's Grand Coalition
Hugenberg leader of DNVP
Kellogg–Briand Pact.
1929 Young Plan
Death of Stresemann
Wall Street Crash

As we saw in the last chapter, during the immediate post-war period the German experiment in parliamentary democracy faced major economic and social problems as well as challenges from both the political left and the political right. Yet the Weimar Republic survived. The years 1924–9 saw an apparent change in fortune and this period has come to be regarded as the high point of the Weimar Republic. It was a glorious, if short-lived, interlude between the early years of crisis and its eventual decline and collapse. It was a time when the term 'the golden twenties' might have been applied to Germany and actually have had a ring of truth about it.

William Shirer, the European correspondent of the American newspaper, the *Chicago Tribune*, reported his impressions of Germany at that time:

1 I was stationed in Paris and occasionally in London at that time, and fas-
   cinating though those capitals were ... they paled a little when one
   came to Berlin and Munich. A wonderful ferment was working in
   Germany. Life seemed more free, more modern, more exciting than in
5 any place I had ever seen. Nowhere else did the arts or the intellectual
   life seem so lively. In contemporary writing, painting, architecture, in
   music and drama, there were new currents and fine talents. And every-
   where there was an accent on youth ... They were a healthy, carefree,
   sun worshipping lot, and they were filled with an enormous zest for
10 living life to the full and in complete freedom. The old oppressive
   Prussian spirit seemed to be dead and buried. Most Germans one met
   – politicians, writers, editors, artists, professors, students, businessmen,
   labour leaders – struck you as being democratic, liberal, even pacifist.

The rosy image of Weimar in the mid-1920s is not false since this
middle period of the 1920s witnessed a number of notable successes.
However, some historians have come to question the true extent of
Weimar Republic's health and stability at this time. If Germany was
really on the road to economic recovery and political stability, how
was it that it all fell apart so soon after the start of the world
depression triggered by the Wall Street Crash in 1929?

1 The Economic Situation

> **KEY ISSUE** To what extent was German economic recovery
> soundly based and likely to last?

a) Economic recovery?

It is sometimes claimed that the introduction of a new currency, the
Rentenmark, and the measures brought about by the Dawes Plan ush-
ered in five years of economic growth and affluence. It is said that
the period stands out in marked contrast to the economic chaos of
1922–3, and was only brought to an end by the world depression of
1929–3. Certainly, for contemporaries looking back at the end of the
1920s, it seemed as if Germany had made a remarkable recovery.
In 1929 the economist W.A. Angell published a book entitled
The Recovery of Germany. The book contains a report sent to
the Reparations Committee in December 1922 by Gilbert Parker, the
American financier and the Agent for Reparation Payments:

1 German business conditions generally appear to have righted themselves on a relatively high level of activity. A year ago, it will be recalled,
   German business was in the midst of a process of expansion which
   threatened to result in over-production in certain of the principal indus-
5 tries ... As the year 1928 comes to a close, it appears that this over-
   expansion has been checked before it reached dangerous proportions,

and that a condition of relative stability has been achieved ... Since 1924, when stabilisation was achieved and the execution of the Experts' Plan began, Germany's reconstruction has at least kept pace with the
10 reconstruction of Europe as a whole, and it has played an essential part in the process of European reconstruction.

In spite of the loss of resources as a result of the Treaty of Versailles, heavy industry was able to recover reasonably quickly and, by 1928, production levels exceeded those of 1913. This was the result of the use of more efficient methods of production, particularly in coal-mining and steel manufacture, and also the investment of foreign capital. Foreign investors were attracted to Germany because of its high interest rates. At the same time, German industry enjoyed the advantages of the economies of scale brought about by the growing number of cartels. IG Farben, the chemicals giant, became the largest manufacturing enterprise in Europe, whilst Vereinigte Stahlweeke combined the coal, iron and steel interests of Germany's great industrialists and grew to control nearly half of all production. Between 1925 and 1929, German exports rose by 40 per cent. Such economic progress brought social benefits as well. Hourly wage rates rose every year from 1924 to 1930 and by as much as five to ten per cent in 1927 and 1928. There were also striking improvements in the provision of social welfare. A generous pensions and sickness benefits scheme was started whilst, in 1927, compulsory unemployment insurance covering 17 million workers was introduced. It was the largest scheme of its kind in the world. In addition, state subsidies were provided for the construction of local amenities such as parks, schools, sports facilities and especially council housing. All these developments alongside the more obvious signs of wealth, such as the increasing number of cars and the growth of the cinema, supported the view that the Weimar Republic's economy was enjoying boom conditions.

However, the actual rate of German recovery was unclear. There was economic growth, but it was uneven and in 1926 production actually declined. In overseas trade, the value of imports always exceeded those of exports. Unemployment never fell below 1.3 million in this period and even before the effects of America's financial crisis began to be felt, in 1929, the number of unemployed averaged 1.9 million. In agriculture, grain production was still only three-quarters of its 1913 figure and farmers, many of whom were in debt, faced falling incomes. By the late 1920s, income per head in agriculture was 44 per cent below the national average. What were the reasons for these economic problems? Why were they so serious as to represent a long-term threat to the German economy?

b) Economic problems persist – 'a crisis before the crisis'

Firstly, world economic conditions did not favour Germany which had traditionally depended on its exports for growth. World trade did not return to pre-war levels and, hindered by protective tariffs, German exports, as a share of the total amount of goods and services produced in a year, declined. German exports were also handicapped by the loss of valuable territories such as Alsace-Lorraine and Silesia by the Treaty of Versailles. German agriculture also found itself in difficulties because of world economic conditions. The fall in world prices from the mid-1920s placed a great strain on farmers who made up one-third of the population. Support in the form of government financial aid and tariffs could only partially help to reduce the problems. Such payments were likely to add to the country's economic and political burdens. Most significantly, this decline in income reduced the spending power of a large section of the population and this led to a fall in demand within the economy as a whole. A further problem was the changing balance of the population. From the mid-1920s, those who were part of the pre-war increase in the birth rate reached school leaving age and so increased the available workforce from 32.4 million in 1925 to 33.4 million in 1931. This meant that even without a recession, there was always likely to be an increase in unemployment in Germany. Rates of investment and savings were also not encouraging. Savers had lost a great deal of money in the post-war inflation and, after 1924, there was little enthusiasm to invest money again. Starved of investment, the German economy came to rely on investors from abroad, who were attracted by the prospect of higher interest rates than they could earn in their own countries. As a result, Germany's economic well-being became even more dependent on foreign investment over which it had no control and which might not continue into the future. Government finances also gave cause for concern. Although the government succeeded in balancing the budget in 1924, from 1925 it continually ran into debt but even so, it continued to spend increasing sums of money. By 1928 public expenditure had reached 26 per cent of gross national product which was double the pre-war figure. The government, unable to make good this debt by encouraging domestic savings, was forced to rely more and more on international loans. Such a situation did not provide the basis for future economic growth. In its annual report of 1927, the *Deutsche Bank* said:

1   There can in fact be no question of any steady development of our
     economic life as long as the Reparations problem has not been solved
     definitively and in a manner favourable to us. In 1928 it referred to, ...
     the complete inner weakness of our economy. It is so overloaded with
5   taxes required by the excessively expensive apparatus of the state, with
     over-high social payments, and particularly with the reparations sum
     now reaching its 'normal' level [as laid down by the Dawes Plan] that
     any healthy growth is constricted. Development is only possible to the
     extent that these restrictive chains are removed.

All this suggests that, even before the start of the depression, the German economy was already in a very poor state. At the time, the problems were hidden by the flood of foreign capital and by the development of an extensive, but costly, social welfare system. Yet, both these factors were in their own way 'time-bombs' waiting to go off sometime in the future. What remains less clear-cut is exactly how severe the Weimar Republic's economic problems were during this period, and whether they were sufficiently serious to threaten the continued existence of Germany's democracy.

c) The views of Borchardt and Holtfrerich

In the late 1970s, the German economic historian Karl Borchardt was the first to argue that, during the years 1925–9, Germany was living well beyond her means and that her economy was in a serious condition. Not only was public spending out of control, but also wage levels were rising without being matched by increases in production. This, he maintained, was the result of government intervention in the labour market that showed an over-sympathetic attitude towards the trade unions. For example, the introduction of compulsory wage negotiations between employers and the unions and the higher contributions required from employers towards social insurance both increased production costs and left less money available for investment. This slowed economic growth. By 1927–8, the prospect of falling profits had so badly affected business that there were already signs that 'points were set to depression'. His assessment of the Weimar Republic's economy concluded that it was 'an abnormal, in fact a sick economy, which could not possibly have gone on in the same way, even if the world depression had not occurred'. Borchardt's views proved to be controversial and were not widely accepted.

Another German historian, Carl Holtfrerich, thought differently. His view was that the German economy was not in a weak condition and was only temporarily 'off the rails'. He threw doubt on Borchardt's view that excessive wage increases were at the heart of Weimar Republic's economic problems. He claimed, instead, that the real cause was to be found in the high level of German interest rates that discouraged industrial and agricultural investment but still failed to restore the people's faith in savings. Consequently, investment and growth remained at low levels and there was no means of creating new jobs.

It is now generally recognised that by 1929 the Weimar economy was facing serious problems. Indeed, it seems safe to reach two key conclusions. Firstly, the German economy's dependence on foreign loans made it liable to suffer from any problems that arose in the world economy generally. Secondly, various sectors of the German economy had actually started to slow down from 1927. Whether this amounts to proof of Borchardt's view of a 'sick' economy remains uncertain. Any assessment of what might have happened without a world economic crisis can only be guesswork. However, the evidence tends to suggest that by 1929 the Republic was already facing economic difficulties and was heading for a major economic crisis. In that sense the German economy experienced a 'crisis before the crisis' and America's financial collapse, although important, only added to an already grave situation.

2 Political Recovery

> **KEY ISSUE** Why did the establishment of workable coalition governments prove so difficult?

a) Müller's grand coalition

The election results during the middle years of the Weimar Republic give grounds for cautious optimism about its long-term survival (see the results for 1924 and 1928 in the table on page 135). The extremist parties of both left and right lost ground and altogether polled less than 30 per cent of the votes cast. The DNVP peaked in December 1924 with 103 seats (20.5 per cent) and fell back to 73 (14.2 per cent) in May 1928. The Nazis lost ground in both elections and were reduced to only 12 seats (2.6 per cent) by 1928. The KPD, although recovering slightly by 1928 with 54 seats (10.6 per cent), remained below their performance of May 1924 and well below the combined votes gained by the KPD and USPD in June 1920. On the other hand, the parties sympathetic to the Republic maintained their share of the vote or, as in the case of the SPD, made substantial gains winning 153 seats (29.8 per cent) in 1928. Following the 1928 election, a 'Grand Coalition' of the SPD, DDP, DVP and Centre was formed under Hermann Müller, the leader of the SPD. It enjoyed the support of over 60 per cent of the *Reichstag* and it seemed as if democracy was at last beginning to emerge in Weimar politics.

However, the election of 1928 must not be regarded as typical in Weimar history and should not be allowed to hide the continuing basic weaknesses of the German parliamentary and party system. These were not only the problems created by proportional representation, but also the ongoing difficulty of creating coalitions from amongst the various parties and then maintaining them when party differences emerged. In such situations each party tended to put its own self-interest before those of the government.

b) Party differences and lack of co-operation

The parties continued to reflect their traditional interests of religious denomination or class and attempts to widen their appeal made little progress. As a result, the differences between the main parties meant that opportunities to form workable coalitions were very limited.

There was never any possibility of a coalition including both the SPD and the DNVP, and the Communist KPD remained totally isolated. A right-centre coalition of Centre, DVP and DNVP created a situation in which the parties tended to agree on domestic issues but disagree on foreign affairs. On the other hand, a broad coalition of SPD, DDP, DVP and Centre meant that the parties agreed on foreign policy but differed on domestic issues. A minority government of the political centre, including the DDP, DVP and Centre could only exist by seeking support from either the left or right. It was impossible to create a coalition with a parliamentary majority that could also consistently agree on both domestic and foreign policy. In this situation, there was very little chance of democratic government being able to establish any lasting political stability. Of the seven governments between 1924 and 1930, only two had majorities and the longest survived 21 months. In fact, the only reason governments lasted as long as they did was because the opposition parties were also unable or unwilling to unite. More often than not, it was conflicts within the parties that formed the coalition governments that led them to their collapse.

The attitude of the Weimar Republic's political parties towards parliamentary government was irresponsible. This may well have been the legacy from imperial times when their limited role had only allowed them to express their own narrow party interests in the knowledge that it was the Kaiser who ultimately decided policy. However, in the 1920s, parliamentary democracy needed the political parties to show a more responsible attitude towards government. The evidence suggests that even in the most stable period of the Republic's history no such attitude existed.

For example, until 1932 the socialist SPD was the largest party in the *Reichstag*. Although firm in its support of republicanism, it was divided between its desire to uphold the interests of the working class and its commitment to democracy. Some, particularly those on the left of the party and those associated with the trade union movement, feared that working with the *bourgeois* liberal parties would lead to a weakening of the party's commitment to a socialist programme.

Governments of the Weimar Republic, 1923–30.		
Period in office	**Chancellor**	**Make up of the coalition**
1923–24	Wilhelm Marx	Centre, DDP, DVP
1924–25	Wilhelm Marx	Centre, DDP, DVP
1925	Hans Luther	Centre, DVP, DNVP
1926	Hans Luther	Centre, DDP, DVP
1926	Wilhelm Marx	Centre, DDP, DVP
1927–28	Wilhelm Marx	Centre, DDP, DNVP
1928–30	Hermann Müller	SPD, DDP, Centre, DVP

Others, the more moderate, wanted to participate in government in order to ensure it remained sympathetic to its views. At the same time, the old argument between those who favoured gradual reform and the more militant Marxists (see page 102) continued to hinder the party. As a result, the SPD found itself in a defensive position during the middle years of the Republic and it did not join any of the government coalitions until 1928. Then, almost immediately, Hermann Müller, the SPD Chancellor, faced criticism from his own party on a relatively minor issue – the construction of one armoured cruiser.

c) The role of the Centre Party

It therefore fell to the Centre Party to provide the political lead. The Centre Party backed all the governments from 1919 to 1932 and held ministerial posts in most of them. However, its attempts to bridge the gaps between the social classes and so extend its appeal beyond its traditional Catholic base had only limited success and led to internal quarrels. In the early years, such differences had been put to one side under the left-wing leadership of Matthias Erzberger and Josef Wirth. However, during the 1920s the Party moved decisively to the right and the divisions within the Party became increasingly apparent. In 1928, the leadership eventually passed to Ludwig Kaas and Heinrich Brüning for whom right-wing political partners had more appeal than coalition with the partners who favoured liberalism or social democracy. This was a worrying sign both for the future of the Centre Party and for Germany herself.

The position of the German liberals also left a great deal to be desired. The DDP and DVP joined in all the coalition governments of this period and in Gustav Stresemann, the leader of the DVP, they possessed the Republic's only really inspired statesman. However, this hid some worrying trends. Their share of the vote, though remaining constant in the mid-1920s, had nearly halved since 1919–20, when it had been between 22 and 23 per cent. The reasons for their eventual collapse after 1930 were already to be seen. This decline was largely a result of the divisions within both parties. The DDP lacked clear leadership and its membership was involved in internal bickering over policy. The DVP was also divided and, despite the efforts Stresemann made to bring unity to the Party, this remained a source of conflict. It is not really surprising that moves to bring about some kind of united liberal party came to nothing. As a result, the appeal of German liberalism declined, as was accurately indicated by the decrease of its support among the electorate.

d) The DNVP and the emergence of Hugenberg

One optimistic feature of German party politics came unexpectedly from the conservative DNVP. Since 1919, the DNVP had been totally opposed to the republic and had refused to take part in government. In electoral terms, it had enjoyed considerable success, and in December 1924, gained 103 seats. However, as the Republic began to recover after the 1923 crisis, it became increasingly clear that the DNVP's hopes of restoring a more right-wing government were diminishing and that being continually in opposition would achieve nothing. Some influential groups within the DNVP realised that if they were to have any influence on government policy, then the party had to be prepared to participate in government. As a result, in 1925 and 1927, the DNVP joined government coalitions. This more sympathetic attitude towards the Republic was an encouraging development. However, it was not popular with all groups within the Party. When in the 1928 election, the DNVP vote fell by a quarter, the more extreme right wing were again able to reassert themselves and elect Alfred Hugenberg as the new leader. Hugenberg, who owned 150 newspapers, a publishing house and had interests in the film industry, was Germany's greatest media tycoon. He was an extreme nationalist who utterly rejected the idea of a republic based on parliamentary democracy. He now used all his resources to promote his political message. The DNVP reverted to a programme of total opposition to the Republic and refused to be involved in government. A year later, his party was working closely with the Nazis against the Young Plan.

e) Hindenburg, President of the Republic

One of the factors that contributed to the change of approach by the nationalists was the election of seventy-eight year old Field Marshal Hindenburg as president in 1925. This development may be seen from different viewpoints. On the one hand, on Hindenburg's coming to power there was no immediate swing to the right. The new President proved totally loyal to his constitutional responsibilities and he carried out his presidential duties with correctness. Those nationalists who had hoped that his election might lead to the restoration of the monarchy or the creation of a military-type regime were disappointed. Indeed, it has been argued that with Hindenburg holding the office of President, Germany had at last found its true substitute kaiser or *Ersatzkaiser* and the Republic had at last gained respectability. On the other hand, it is difficult to ignore the pitfalls resulting from the appointment of an old man. In his heart, he had no real sympathy for the Republic or its values. Those around him were mainly made up of anti-republican figures, many of them in the army. He preferred to include the DNVP in government and, if possible, to exclude the SPD. From the start, Hindenburg's view was that the government should move to the right. It was only after 1929 that the serious implications of this for Weimar democracy became fully apparent. As the historian A.J. Nicholls put it: 'he refused to betray the republic, but he did not rally the people to its banner'.

f) Conclusion

It is difficult not to conclude that, during this period, the parliamentary and party political system in Germany failed to make any real progress. It had just coped as best it could. It carried out the work of government but with only limited success. There was no *putsch* from left or right and the anti-republican extremists were contained. Law and order was restored and the activities of the various paramilitary groups were curtailed. However, despite the good intentions of certain individuals and groups, there were no signs of any strengthening of the political structure. Stable government had not been established. This is not surprising when it is remembered that one coalition government fell over such a minor issue as the national flag and another over the creation of denominational schools. Even more significant for the future was the growing contempt and cynicism shown by the people towards party politics and the wheeler-dealing associated with bargaining that led to the creation of most coalitions. The feeling of the people towards the system is most obviously revealed by the declining turn-out at elections (see the table on page 28) and by the growth in the number of small fringe parties. Looking back, the apparent stability of these years was really a deception, a mirage. It misled some people into believing that a genuine basis for lasting stable government had been achieved. It had not.

3 Weimar Foreign Policy

> **KEY ISSUE** To what extent were the aims of German foreign policy related to the bringing about of reconciliation?

a) Background – continued hostility to Versailles

The foreign policy of the Weimar Republic was dominated by a determination to revise the Treaty of Versailles. On no other issue was there such agreement as in the desire to erase the memory of the 'shameful peace'. However, if there was agreement on the basic aim of German foreign policy, a division of opinion existed over how it should be achieved. Those who might be regarded as hardliners believed that the treaty's terms should be resisted wherever possible. They thought that reparations should not be paid, that the disarmament clauses of the treaty should be disregarded and that the territorial clauses should be rejected and overturned. They accepted that a future military conflict with France and her allies was almost unavoidable and that therefore Germany needed to be in a state of military readiness. Typical of such views was Colonel Stülpnagel's memorandum that was sent to the Foreign Office in 1926 with the approval of Hans von Seeckt, the head of the German army or *Reichsweir*:

1 The immediate aim of German policy must be the regaining of full sovereignty over the area retained by Germany, the firm acquisition of those areas at present separated from her, and the re-acquisition of those areas essential to the German economy. That is to say:

5   1. The liberation of the Rhineland and the Saar area.
  2. The abolition of the Corridor and the regaining of Polish Upper Silesia.
  3. The *Anschluss* of German Austria.
  4. The abolition of the Demilitarised Zone.

10 These immediate political aims will produce conflict primarily with France and Belgium and with Poland which is dependent on them, then with Czechoslovakia and finally also with Italy... The above exposition of Germany's political aims... clearly shows that the problem for Germany in the next stages of her political development can only be the re-estab-
15 lishment of her position in Europe, and that the regaining of her world position will be a task for the distant future. Re-establishing a European position is for Germany a question in which land forces will almost exclusively be decisive, for the opponent of this resurrection is in the first place France. It is certainly to be assumed that a reborn Germany will
20 eventually come into conflict with the American-English powers in the struggle for raw materials and markets, and that she will then need adequate maritime forces. But this conflict will be fought out on the basis of a firm European position, after a new solution to the Franco-German problem has been achieved through either peace or war.

The moderates recognised that the weak domestic position of Germany would prevent them pursuing such a foreign policy. For this reason they believed that Germany should follow the twin policies of economic development at home and reconciliation abroad. It was only by working with the Allies that they could hope to reduce the burden of reparations that was holding back the German economy. Further, it was only by restoring Germany's economic strength that Germany could hope to regain her once influential voice in international affairs. This policy of moderate revisionism came to be known as 'fulfilment' and is most closely associated with the names of Josef Wirth, German Chancellor between May 1921 and November 1922, and Gustav Stresemann, Chancellor August–November 1923 and afterwards foreign minister until his death in October 1929.

b) Wirth's 'fulfilment' policy

Wirth's 'fulfilment' policy was extremely unpopular in right-wing nationalist circles and there is little doubt that its supporters became targets in the political violence of the early 1920s. Popular backing for the policy was not helped by the developing inflationary crisis that many Germans put down to the burden of reparations. There was little sympathy from the Allies, since the reparations payments remained so limited. In this sense 'fulfilment' without financial and currency reform proved a failure. Following Wirth's resignation at the end of 1922, the hardliners took control of the Republic's foreign policy.

An important aspect of Wirth's period of office was the signing of the Soviet-German Treaty of Rapallo in April 1922. This was not an alliance, but a treaty of friendship establishing full diplomatic relations between the two countries. In addition, it was agreed that they would drop all claims for war damage and reparations against each other whilst secret clauses arranged for future collaboration in military matters. At the time, the Allies were horrified by what they regarded as an 'unholy alliance'. It was seen as a German-led conspiracy against the Versailles settlement. It is certainly true that hardliners in the army and the foreign office supported a pro-Soviet policy. They believed that an improvement in Russo-German relations would reduce the need for 'fulfilment' with the Allies. It might also result in combined military action against Poland and the downfall of the entire Versailles settlement. However, those historians who have seen such motives as guiding German foreign policy have tended to play up the significance of the hardliners and disregarded the influence of the key figures such as Wirth and Rathenau. These regarded the Treaty of Rapallo as part of a broader plan. Certainly, they wanted Germany to escape from the isolation of the post-war years and they wanted to counterbalance the French influence in Europe but they never intended that the treaty should be pursued in isolation and at the expense of 'fulfilment'. They considered Rapallo in the east as going hand in hand with 'fulfilment' in the west.

Wirth's foreign policy brought only limited success. During the disaster of 1923, foreign policy was controlled by the hardliners who started a policy of 'passive resistance'. Though such a policy may have satisfied certain nationalistic views, the limitations of that approach were highlighted by the events of 1923. With the reparations problem not solved, Germany lapsed into a period of hyper-inflation. Those German diplomats and politicians who had hoped to be able to make a stand against the Allies and Versailles only succeeded in highlighting Germany's military and diplomatic weakness which even friendship with the USSR could not hide. In August 1923, at the height of the crisis, Stresemann was appointed chancellor and the policy of 'fulfilment' was restored.

4 The Stresemann Years

> **KEY ISSUE** What were the real aims of Stresemann's foreign policy?

a) Contradictory views

The emergence of Gustav Stresemann, regarded by many as the

Weimar Republic's only statesman of quality, has long been the focus of controversy. A study of both his character and his political views has resulted in a wide range of differing interpretations. He has been regarded as both a fanatical nationalist and a 'great European' working for international reconciliation. He has been praised for his staunch support of parliamentary government and also condemned for pretending to be a democrat. He has been portrayed as an idealist on the one hand and an opportunist on the other.

These contradictory opinions have arisen since new documentary sources became available. As a result, views about his career and his achievements have changed. Following his early death in 1929, most assessments of Stresemann were favourable. However, after 1933 his reputation was blackened by Nazi historians, whilst in western Europe the publication of some private letters raised doubts about the sincerity of his foreign policy. Some German historians portray him as a prophet of European unity who stood in sharp contrast to those who championed German expansionism. Such a view became unacceptable after the publication of his private papers and diaries and disclosures made in German Foreign Office files in the 1950s. Afterwards, interpretations have tended to show him as the hard-headed German nationalist with a subtle grasp of power politics.

This wide range of interpretations has also come about because of the chequered nature of Stresemann's political career. Before 1921–2, there was little to suggest that Stresemann was to become the mainstay of a democratic republic. In the years before 1914, his nationalism found expression in his support of *Weltpolitik* and his membership of the Navy League. During the First World War, Stresemann was an ardent supporter of the *Siegfriede* (see page 81). He campaigned for unrestricted submarine warfare, opposed the 'peace resolution' and was part of the conspiracy that led to the downfall Bethmann-Hollweg. By 1918 his support for the military and its imposition of the Treaty of Brest–Litovsk on Russia had earned him the title of 'Ludendorff's young man'. As a result, in 1919, after the break-up of the National Liberals, he was deliberately excluded from the DDP. He was left no real option but to form his own party, the DVP. The party was hostile to the revolution and the Republic and campaigned for the restoration of the monarchy. Indeed, it was only after the failed Kapp *Putsch* and the murders of Erzberger and Rathenau that Stresemann led his party into adopting a more sympathetic stance towards the Republic. His sudden change of heart that turned him into a *Vernunftrepublikaner,* a rational republican, has provided plenty of evidence for those critics who have regarded his support of the Weimar Republic as pretence. This charge is not entirely fair. His career during the war years has tended to overshadow his strong opposition to the self-interest of the conservatives and his support for moves towards constitutional government in the years before 1914. Ideally, Stresemann would have liked a parliamentary-based constitutional monarchy. That was not to be. By 1922 he had become convinced that the Republic and its constitution provided Germany with its only chance of preventing the dictatorship of either left or right. This was quite simply his realistic assessment of the situation. It cannot fairly be claimed that it was a decision reached because of a desire to become more popular or to advance his own career further.

b) Stresemann and foreign affairs

From the time he became responsible for foreign affairs at the height of the 1923 crisis, Stresemann's foreign policy was shaped by his deep understanding of the domestic and international situations. Unlike many nationalists, he recognised that Germany had been militarily defeated and not simply 'stabbed in the back'. He rejected the solutions of those hardliners who failed to understand the circumstances that had brought Germany to its knees in 1923. However, none of this is to deny that Stresemann's main aims were to free Germany from the shackles of Versailles and to restore his country to the status of a great power, the equal of Britain and France. Indeed, it has been said that the ideas of Stresemann's foreign policy were derived from Germany's pre-1914 ambitions. In a private letter to the ex-Crown Prince in September 1927 Stresemann wrote:

> 1 In my opinion there are three great tasks that confront German foreign policy in the more immediate future: – In the first place the solution of the Reparations question in a sense tolerable for Germany and the assurance of peace, which is an essential premise for the recovery of
> 5 our strength. Secondly, the protection of Germans abroad, those 10 to 12 millions of our kindred who now live under a foreign yoke in foreign lands. The third great task is the readjustment of our eastern frontiers; the recovery of Danzig, the Polish Corridor, and a correction of the frontier in Upper Silesia. In the background stands the union with
> 10 German Austria, although I am quite clear that this not merely brings no advantages to Germany, but seriously complicates the problem of the German Reich... The question of a choice between east and west does not arise as the result of our joining the League. Such a choice can only be made when backed by military force. That, alas we do not pos-
> 15 sess. We can neither become a continental spearhead for England, as some believe, nor can we involve ourselves in an alliance with Russia. I would utter warning against any utopian ideas of coquetting (flirting) with Bolshevism.

Since offensive action was out of the question, Stresemann's only remaining choice was diplomacy. How could he achieve his aims in the 1920s when, as he himself once remarked, he was only backed up by the power of German culture and the German economy? Firstly, he was prepared to recognise that France did rightly have security concerns and that France also controlled the balance of power on the continent. He regarded Franco-German friendship as essential to solving outstanding problems. Secondly, in order to earn the goodwill and co-operation of Britain and the USA, both of whom were able to exert influence on France, he played on Germany's importance to world trade. The sympathy of the USA was also vital in order to attract American investment into the German economy. Thirdly, he wished to maintain the Rapallo-based friendship with the USSR. He rejected out of hand those hardliners who desired an alliance with Soviet Russia and described them as the 'maddest of foreign policy makers'. Stresemann's strategy was in the tradition of Wirth's fulfilment. He was a moderate revisionist. In the long term, he wanted Germany to be the leading power in Europe once again. To that end, he saw co-operation and peace, particularly with the Western powers, as being in the best interests of Germany.

The starting point of Stresemann's foreign policy was the issue of reparations. As Chancellor he had called off 'passive resistance' and agreed to resume the payment of reparations. The result of this was the relief brought by the American backed Dawes Plan.

THE DAWES PLAN

The reorganisation of German currency. One new *Reichsmark* was to be worth one billion of the old.

The setting up of a German national bank, the *Reichsbank,* under Allied supervision.

An international loan of 800 million gold marks to aid German economic recovery. The loan was to be financed mainly by the United States.

New arrangements for the payment of reparations. Payment to be made annually at a fixed scale over a longer period.

Although the plan left the actual sum to be paid unchanged, it based the monthly instalments over the first five years according to Germany's capacity to pay. Furthermore, it provided for a large loan to Germany to aid economic recovery. The Dawes Plan has been described as 'a victory for financial realism' and all interested parties accepted it in July 1924. For Stresemann, its advantages were many. For the first time, Germany's economic problems received international recognition. It gained credit by means of the loan and subsequent investments for the cash-starved German economy; and it resulted in a French promise to evacuate the Ruhr during 1925. In the short term the Dawes Plan was a success. The German economy was not weakened, since it imported twice as much capital as it paid out in reparations. The mere fact that reparations were being paid

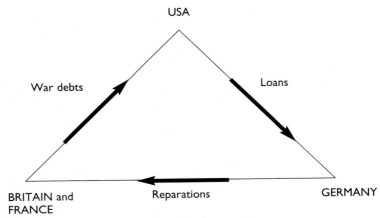

Reparations, war debts and loans

regularly contributed to the improved relations between France and Germany during these years. However, the whole system was dangerously dependent on the continuation of American loans, since they paid German reparations which, in turn, were used to settle Allied war debts. In attempting to break out of the crisis of 1923 Stresemann had unwittingly linked Germany's fortunes to powerful external forces the danger of which was to become apparent after 1929.

c) Locarno, 1925

The ending of the occupation of the Ruhr and the introduction of the Dawes Plan showed that the two sides could at least take each other's interests seriously. However, Stresemann continued to fear that Anglo-French friendship could lead to an alliance, especially if France began to feel threatened by Germany's industrial recovery. In order to counter such a development, in early 1925 Stresemann proposed a security pact for Germany's western frontiers. Although France was at first hesitant, Britain and the USA both backed the idea. This formed the basis for the Locarno Pact signed in October 1925. By the treaty, Germany, France and Belgium agreed to respect their existing frontiers, including the demilitarised Rhineland. Britain and Italy guaranteed these terms. By the treaties, Germany, Poland and Czechoslovakia agreed to settle future disputes peacefully, but the existing frontiers were not accepted as final. The Locarno treaties represented an important diplomatic development. Germany was freed from its isolation by the Allies and was again treated as an equal partner. In fact, Stresemann had achieved a great deal at Locarno at very little cost. He had confirmed the existing frontiers in the west, since Germany was in no position to do otherwise. In so doing he had also limited France's freedom of action since the occupation of the Ruhr or the annexation of the Rhineland were no longer possibilities. Moreover, by establishing a solid basis for Franco-German understanding, Stresemann had lessened the urgency of the French search for security and her need to find allies elsewhere in Europe. The Poles viewed the treaties as a major setback, since Stresemann had deliberately refused to confirm the frontiers in the east. Stresemann hoped that further advances would follow Locarno. He hoped for the early restoration of full German rule over the Saar and the Rhineland, a reduction in reparations; and then later, possibly, a revision of the eastern frontier.

In the years immediately after Locarno there was further diplomatic progress. In 1926, Germany joined the League of Nations and two years later she signed the Kellogg–Briand Pact, a declaration that outlawed 'war as an instrument of national policy'. Finally, in 1929 the Allies agreed to evacuate the Rhineland earlier than intended in return for a final settlement of the reparations issue. The result was the Young Plan, which further revised the scheme of payments. Germany now agreed to continue to pay reparations until 1988 although the total sum was reduced to £1,850 million, only one-quarter of the figure demanded in 1921.

Although Stresemann viewed friendship with the West as his priority, he was also determined to stay on good terms with the USSR. As a result, the two countries signed the Treaty of Berlin in April 1926 in order to continue the basis of the relationship first established at Rapallo. This was not double-dealing by Stresemann but was simply a recognition that, because of her position in the heart of Europe, Germany's defence requirements needed her to reach agreements with both East and West. The treaty with the Soviet Union reduced fears, opened up the possibility of a large commercial market, and placed even more pressure on Poland to give way to German demands for frontier changes.

d) Assessment

In 1926, along with his British and French counterparts Aristide Briand and Austen Chamberlain, Stresemann was awarded the Nobel Peace Prize. Three years later, at the early age of 51, he died suddenly of a heart attack. The socialist newspaper, *Vorwärts*, wrote in its obituary column:

1   Stresemann's achievement was in line with the ideas of the international socialist movement. He saw that you can only serve your people by understanding other peoples. To serve collapsed Germany he set out on the path of understanding. He refused to try to get back land, which had
5   gone forever. He offered our former enemies friendship. Being a practical man he saw that any other path would have left Germany without any hope of recovery. He covered the long distance from being a nationalist politician of conquest to being a champion of world peace. He fought with great personal courage for the ideals in which he believed

10 ... It is no wonder that right-wingers watched with horror as he went from his original camp to the opposite one. They could not accept him because doing so involved accepting that the Republic created by the workers had brought Germany from devastation to recovery.

There can be little doubt that Stresemann achieved a great deal in a short time to change both Germany's domestic and international positions. Moreover, the improvement had been achieved by peaceful methods. When one also considers the dire situation he inherited in 1923 with forces, both internal and external, stacked against him, it is perhaps not surprising that his policy has been described by the leading German historian of the Weimar Republic, E. Kolb, as 'astonishingly successful'. However, it should be borne in mind that circumstances worked strongly in Stresemann's favour. From 1924 to 1929, changes in the international situation and the coming of economic prosperity were important factors in the shaping of events. Stresemann has also been criticised for over-estimating the potential of his policy of establishing friendly relations with other powers. The limits and slow pace of the changes that he hoped for caused him disappointment. By the time of his death, the nationalist opposition was mobilising itself against the Young Plan and there was a growing feeling that Stresemann's policy of conciliation was coming to an end. It must be questioned whether Stresemann could ever have achieved his aims, particularly with regard to the issue of the Polish frontier. As it was, his death and the onset of the world depression were followed by the collapse of the Republic. In the years after 1929, Stresemann's policies gave way to a harder line that ended in the aggressive foreign policy of Hitler's Third Reich. The distinction is an important one. For whatever the limitations of Stresemann's policy, his vision of Germany as a great power was founded upon the ideas of international peace and negotiated settlements. Like Bismarck, Stresemann recognised the importance of peace for Germany in the realm of international affairs. His achievement was indeed considerable, although by 1929 his policy had not lasted long enough to survive the different circumstances of the 1930s.

5 The Weimar Republic, 1924–9 – An Overview

> **KEY ISSUE** Just how stable was the Weimar Republic during this period?

The years 1924–9 mark the high point of the Weimar Republic. By comparison with the periods of crisis before and after, these years do appear stable. The real increase in prosperity experienced by many and the cultural vitality of the period both give support to the view that these years were indeed 'the golden twenties'. However, historians have generally tended to qualify this stability. Kolb describes these

Der Retter Stresemann –
The Saviour
Stresemann. A German
cartoon portrays
Stresemann as the
guardian angel of the
young Republic.

years as ones of 'relative stabilisation' and Peukert describes them as years of 'deceptive stability'. This is because the stability was in actual fact limited in scope.

Germany's economic recovery was built on unstable foundations that created a false idea of prosperity. Problems persisted in the economy and they were only hidden by an increasing reliance on credit from abroad. In this way Germany's future economic stability became tied up with powerful external forces over which it had no control. Hindsight, therefore, now allows historians to see that, in the late twenties, any disruption to the world's trading pattern or its financial markets was bound to have a particularly damaging effect on the uncertain German economy. German society was still divided by deep class differences as well as by regional and denominational differences that prevented the development of national agreement and harmony. The war and the years of crisis that followed had left the remains of feelings of bitterness, fear and resentment between employers and their workers. Following the introduction of the state scheme for settling disputes in 1924, its procedure was used as a matter of course when the intention had been that its use would be the exception not the rule. As a result, some 76,000 industrial disputes were considered between 1924 and 1932. In 1928, workers were locked out from their place of work in the Ruhr ironworks when the employers refused to accept the arbitration award. It was the most serious industrial confrontation of the Weimar period. It showed the extent of the bitterness of industrial relations even before the start of the world depression. The lack of agreement was also to be seen in the political sphere where the parliamentary system had failed to build on the changes of 1918. The original ideals of the constitution had not been developed and there was little sign that the system had produced a stable and mature political system. In particular, the main democratic parties had still not recognised the necessity of working together in a spirit of compromise. It was not so much the weaknesses of the constitution such as the existence of proportional representation that produced so many political parties or the short-lived coalitions which created the main political problems, but the failure to establish a widely-respected political outlook which would be able to withstand a future crisis. Even the successes of Stresemann in the field of foreign affairs have to be offset by the fact that significant numbers of his fellow countrymen at the time rejected his policy out of hand and pressed for a more hardline approach.

Working on Chapter 8

In this chapter you have examined the extent to which the economy recovered and political stability was restored in the Weimar Republic between 1924 and 1928. You may have concluded that, in reality, these middle years of the Republic were only stable when compared to the periods before and after. Why was this? These were certainly years of challenge for the Republic. To what extent were they successful in dealing with the problems that persisted even during these years? You will need to consider which of these problems were inherited from the war and the years of crisis that followed. In addition, which problems were new and a consequence of a lack of political maturity? Finally, can you already identify the reasons why, during the economic and political turmoil that lay ahead, the Weimar system would not be strong enough to withstand the storm?

In Chapters 7 and 8, you will have encountered many words and phrases that are part of the study of economics. Complete the chart below to make sure that you have totally mastered their meanings.

Answering structured and source-based questions on Chapter 8

1. **a)** During the 1920s, which German political parties might have been considered 'sympathetic to the Republic'? (*3 marks*)
   b) What were the differences in the policies of the SPD and KPD? (*5 marks*)
   c) What impact did the leadership of Alfred Hugenberg have on the DNVP? (*5 marks*)
   d) In what sense were the behaviour of Weimar Republic's political parties be considered 'irresponsible'? (*7 marks*)

Summary Diagram
Weimar: Relative Stability, 1924–9

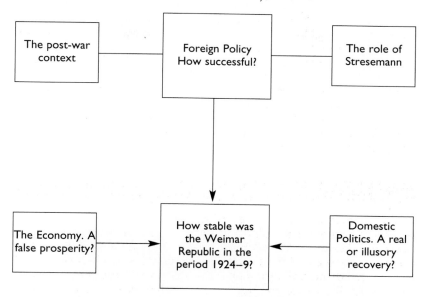

Word or phrase	Meaning
balance of payments	
black market	
deficit financing	
economies of scale	
fixed incomes	
hyperinflation	
national debt	
tariffs	

2. a) What is meant by a policy of 'fulfilment'? (*5 marks*)
   b) What advantages did the Weimar Republic gain from agreeing to the Treaty of Rapallo in 1922? (*5 marks*)
   c) What dangers were inherent in the Dawes Plan? (*5 marks*)
   d) By 1928, in what sense might it have been correct to say that the prosperity of the Weimar Republic was 'built on unstable foundations'? (*5 marks*)

SOURCE A.

A Low cartoon of 1925 shows Briand, Chamberlain and Stresemann agreeing to the Locarno Treaties.

SOURCE B.

1 Stresemann's own motives in concluding these treaties have been subject to much speculation... After his death, sections of his diaries and
papers were published, and it was not surprising that the editors selec-
ted those, which reinforced the picture of Stresemann the peacemaker,
5 Stresemann the good European. With German defeat in the Second
World War, a great deal more evidence became available – much of it
from the files of the German foreign office. It became clear that at the
same time as he was trying to improve relations with the West,
Stresemann was also expressing strongly nationalistic points of view ...
10 There was nothing surprising about these revelations, Stresemann had
always been a German nationalist... His career in the First World War
and after it demonstrated this.
(From *Weimar and the Rise of Hitler* by A.J. Nicholls, 1968.)

SOURCE C.

1 The Treaty could, however, be looked upon from another point of view
and awkward questions asked. If Germany really meant to observe the
Versailles Treaty, which she had signed... ought Locarno to have been
necessary. By agreeing to negotiate with Germany were the other
5 powers in effect accepting the idea that she was not bound by the
Treaty of Versailles? Why should the western frontier of Germany need
a further guarantee?
(From *Europe 1898–1955* by T.J.P. York, 1969.)

SOURCE D.

But the treaties were criticised at the time and ever since on the
grounds that they made one set of European frontiers more inviolable
than others... But the very fact that certain sections of the Versailles
settlement had been given a privileged position weakened the rest of it.
The illusion of security was soon to be shattered. Locarno, in a sense,
reflected the brief period of prosperity that Europe enjoyed up to 1929.
This prosperity died with the Wall Street Crash and so did the spirit of
Locarno. (From *Modern European History* by K. Perry, 1976.)

a) Compare Sources A and B. To what extent do they cast doubt on
Stresemann's motives at Locarno? (*5 marks*)

b) Study Sources C and D. To what extent do the authors question the
value of the Locarno Treaties? (*5 marks*)

c) How full an understanding do the sources provide of the issues
raised by the Locarno Treaties? (*10 marks*)

Essay-type questions on Chapter 8

1. 'The Weimar Republic's only really inspired statesman.' How valid is this
assessment of Gustav Stresemann? (*25 marks*)

2. What progress had the governments of the Weimar Republic made
towards achieving economic and political stability by 1928? Explain your
answer fully. (*25 marks*)

Weimar: The Final Years, 1929–33

POINTS TO CONSIDER

Finally, in the narrative of events, we come to the years of crisis that led to the collapse of the Weimar Republic and with it the rise to power of Hitler and the Nazi Party. The first thing to consider is the Wall Street Crash. Why did it have such a detrimental impact on Germany? Why did it lead to a return of the economic difficulties and political instability evident in the early 1920s? Can all the economic difficulties be blamed on the Crash? Carefully study the years of political crises that led to Hindenburg taking advantage of Clause 48 of the Constitution and introducing presidential government based on rule by decree. You will note that this was the consequence of both political intrigue that made democratic government impossible and the increase in the support for parties of the extreme left and right. Most significant was the growth in the popularity of Hitler and the Nazi Party. Why did this happen? Finally, consider the overriding issue – was the collapse of the Weimar Republic inevitable? It is this question that is the real focus of this chapter.

KEY DATES

1929	Mar	Young Plan approved by *Reichstag*
	Jul	DNVP and Nazis joined forces
	Oct	Stresemann died
	Oct	Wall Street Crash
		Hindenburg authorised the budget by decree
1930	Mar	Resignation of Müller's government
	Jul	Presidential decree used to introduce new economic measures
	Sep	Election – Nazis second largest party in *Reichstag*
1931	May	Leading German banks failed
		Worsening economic crisis as unemployment reached four and a half million
	Oct	Formation of Hartzburg Front
1932		Bruning refused to continue with reparations payments
	Apr	Hindenburg re-elected President of Germany
	May	Brüning resigned. Von Papen appointed Chancellor
	Jul	Elections. Nazis largest party in *Reichstag*
	Nov	Elections. Nazis lost 34 seats
	Dec	Von Papen's ministry collapsed
		Schleicher appointed Chancellor
1933	Jan	Schleichers' ministry collapsed
		Hindenburg appointed Hitler as Chancellor

1 The World Economic Crisis

> **KEY ISSUE** Why did the world economic crisis have such a devastating impact on Germany?

a) The impact of the Wall Street Crash on Germany

There is no dispute amongst historians that the world economic crisis was an event of major significance. The crisis was felt throughout the world and it affected Germany in a particularly savage way. The main issue that arises is whether or not it should be considered the direct cause of Weimar's collapse. Germany was probably more likely to suffer the consequences of the Wall Street Crash, the collapse of share prices on the New York stock exchange in 1929, than any other country. Almost immediately the American loans and investment dried up and this was quickly followed by demands for the repayment of those loans that had previously been provided so willingly. At the same time, the crisis caused a further decline in the prices of food and raw materials as the industrialised nations reduced their imports. The knock-on effects of this affected the industrialised countries, since other countries could no longer afford to import their manufactured goods. As the demand for exports collapsed, so world trade slumped. In this situation, German industry could no longer pay its way. Without the support of overseas loans and with its export trade falling, prices and wages fell and the number of bankruptcies increased.

b) Levels of unemployment

During the winter of 1929–30, unemployment rose above 2 million and only 12 months after the Crash, it had reached 3 million. By September 1932 it stood at 5.1 million. It peaked in early 1933, when 6.1 million Germans were without work. On their own, such figures can provide only a limited understanding of the effects of a slump of this magnitude. Unemployment figures, for example, do not take into account those who did not register. Nor do they record the extent of part-time working throughout German industry.

c) Social impact

Above all, statistics fail to convey the extent of the human suffering that was the consequence of this disaster because the depression in Germany affected virtually everyone and few families escaped its effects. Many manual workers, both skilled and unskilled, faced the prospect of indefinite unemployment. For their wives, there was the impossible task of trying to feed families and keep homes warm on the money provided by limited social security benefits. However, such problems were not limited to the working class. The depression also badly affected the middle classes. From the small shopkeepers to the well-qualified professionals in law and medicine, people struggled to survive in a world where there was little demand for their goods and services. For such, the decline in their economic position was made more difficult by the loss of pride and respectability that accompanied the onset of poverty. In the countryside the situation was no better than in the towns. As world demand fell further, the agricultural depression deepened and this led to widespread rural poverty. For some tenant farmers there was even the ultimate humiliation of being evicted from their homes which had often been in their families for generations.

In the more prosperous times we live in today, it is difficult to appreciate the scale of the suffering that struck German people in the early 1930s. With one-third of the people on the dole, to many ordinary respectable Germans it must have seemed as if society itself was breaking down. The city of Cologne could not pay the interest on its debts, banks closed their doors and in Berlin large crowds of unemployed youngsters were kept occupied with open-air games of chess and cards! In such a situation, it is perhaps not surprising that people lost faith in the Weimar Republic and saw salvation in the solutions offered by other political parties, particularly those on the extreme right and left. However, it is important that this atmosphere of impending disaster is put into some kind of context. The point has already been made that the Weimar economy, even during its period of 'relative stabilisation', faced many problems. This suggests that the world economic crisis should really be seen as simply the final push that brought the Weimar Republic crashing down. Comparisons with other industrialised nations suggest that placing the blame for the world economic crisis on the consequences of the Wall Street Crash is too simple an explanation. The impact of the depression in Germany was certainly more severe than in either Britain or France, but it was on a par with the American experience. In Germany, 1 in 3 workers were unemployed in 1933 and industrial production by 1932 had fallen by 42 per cent of its 1929 level. In the USA, the comparable figures were 1 in 4 and 46 per cent. In spite of such similarities, the USA was never faced with the possibility of a wholesale collapse of its political system. On the other hand, in Germany the economic crisis quickly became a political crisis simply because there was a lack of confidence that weakened the Republic's position in its hour of need. Taken together these two points suggest that the Great Depression speeded up the end of the Weimar Republic, but only because its existing economic circumstances were already very difficult and the democratic basis of its government was not sufficiently well established.

Governments of the Weimar Republic, 1930–33.		
Period in office	**Chancellor**	**Type of government**
1930–31	Heinrich Brüning	Presidential government
1931–32	Heinrich Brüning	Presidential government
1932	Franz von Papen	Presidential government
1932–33	Kurt von Schleicher	Presidential government

On 30 January 1933 Adolf Hitler was appointed
Chancellor of Germany.

2 Heinrich Brüning, Chancellor 1930–2

KEY ISSUE Why did it become necessary for Hindenburg to resort to presidential government?

a) The collapse of Müller's Grand Coalition

In 1929, the German government was a Grand Coalition led by Hermann Müller which had been formed after the general election of 1928. Despite being supported by a majority in the *Reichstag*, Müller's government had from the start been subject to severe internal divisions which were further worsened by the drift to the right of the Centre Party and the death of Stresemann. Not surprisingly, it was an issue of government finance that finally brought down the government in March 1930. The sharp increase in the payment of unemployment benefit had led to heavy losses in the insurance scheme. The SPD and the DVP could not agree on how to tackle it. The SPD, as the political representatives of the workers and trade unions, wanted to increase the contributions and to maintain the levels of welfare payments. The DVP, on the other hand, had strong ties with big business. It insisted on reducing benefits in order to cut costs and to balance the budget. In this situation Müller resigned as Chancellor and was replaced by Heinrich Brüning, the leader of the Centre Party.

b) Brüning's ministry

Brüning's response to the growing economic crisis was to propose increased taxes and substantial cuts in government expenditure, but in July 1930 his budget was rejected in the *Reichstag*. In this situation Brüning took advantage of Article 48 of the Constitution and put the proposals into effect by means of an emergency decree signed by the President. The *Reichstag* challenged the legality of this action and voted for the withdrawal of the decree. A position of deadlock had

'Death of Democracy'. A montage of photographs is used to show how the use of Article 48 effectively buried German democracy.

been reached. Brüning therefore asked Hindenburg to dissolve the *Reichstag* and to call an election for September 1930. He was hopeful that in the developing crisis the electorate would be encouraged to back his centre-right coalition. However, the election results proved him to be disastrously wrong. The Nazis who achieved electoral break-through and suddenly became the second largest party in the *Reichstag* with 107 seats made the biggest gains. Brüning's position was now even more difficult and he could only carry on as Chancellor because he retained the support of Hindenburg and because the SPD decided to tolerate his use of Article 48. They did so in order to pro-tect the Republic from the threat of extremists.

c) Views of Brüning's chancellorship

Brüning's appointment as Chancellor has proved to be highly con-troversial, although, over the years, the points of interest have shifted. Initially, the debate concerned the question of Brüning's aims and the nature of his government. Some historians saw him as a sincere statesman struggling in the face of enormous difficulties to save democracy. They believed that his decision to use Article 48 was an understandable reaction to the failure of party government in the crisis and that the real hammer-blow for German democracy came with his dismissal in 1932 rather than with his appointment two years earlier. Others see him as a reactionary, opposed to democracy, who used his position to introduce emergency powers that paved the way for Hitler's dictatorship. In their view Brüning's chancellorship not only marked the first vital step on the road to destroying the republic, but also made possible Hitler's dictatorship.

The original defenders of Brüning were forced to give way as further evidence became available. Most damning of all was the publication after his death in 1970 of Brüning's own *Memoirs, 1918–34*. This established beyond any doubt that he was a conservative and monarchist who had little sympathy for the democratic Republic. He stated that his aims in government were decisively to weaken the *Reichstag* and to re-establish a Bismarckian-type constitution that would ignore the power and influence of the left. To these ends, he was prepared to use the emergency powers of the presidency and to look for backing from the elites of German society.

Therefore, it is now generally accepted that Brüning's appointment did mark a decisive move away from parliamentary government. The office of chancellor, as well as the presidency, was in the hands of someone unsympathetic to democracy. From September 1930, Brüning's miscalculation resulted in a weakening of the *Reichstag* and the emergence of the Nazis as a national political party. It must also be borne in mind that Brüning had been manoeuvred into office by a circle of political schemers including Otto Meissner, the President's state secretary, Oskar von Hindenburg, the President's son, and Major General Kurt von Schleicher, the political voice of the army. They too had lost faith in the democratic process and they saw in Brüning a respectable conservative figure who could lead an authoritarian government backed by the army.

d) Brüning and the depression – the views of Borchardt and Holtfrerich

Brüning's economic policy was at least consistent. Throughout his two years in office he took measures to reduce inflation in an attempt to balance the budget. Government spending was drastically cut and taxes were raised. This led to an increase in the the number of unemployed. After 1945, Brüning was condemned by most historians for at best being weak and at worst being grossly incompetent. It was generally believed that government needed to follow policies that would expand the economy and so counter the effects of depression. By sticking to a policy of cutting back, it was generally believed that

Brüning seriously worsened the situation and made possible the rise of the Nazis.

It is often stated that a historian is a product of his own times. Perhaps then we should not be surprised that in the mid-1970s, when the world once again moved into recession after a quarter-century of growth, the historian, Borchardt, considered Brüning's reputation more sympathetically. Borchardt's work has already been mentioned in the discussion on Weimar's economy. Indeed, Borchardt's assessment of Weimar at that time as being 'abnormal' and 'incurably sick' also forms an important part of his reassessment of Brüning. In simple terms, Borchardt claims that Brüning had no real choice in his economic policy and that there was no feasible alternative to the measures he took. This was partly because of the consequences of the 1920s and meant that the German economy entered the depression with severe weaknesses. In addition to excessively high wage levels and already large government debts, it was in no position to attempt any kind of economic expansion. This would have required either credit from abroad, which would have been linked to strict conditions, or an increase in the money supply from the *Reichsbank*, which would have brought back fears of inflation. Finally, Borchardt argues that even if the money had been available, the real extent of the depression was only realised in the summer of 1931. By that time it was already too late to introduce measures to prevent unemployment rising above six million. In this sense Borchardt sees Brüning as a relatively innocent pawn at the mercy of economic forces.

Borchardt's defence of Brüning has been disputed because it challenged long-established views. Leading the opposition has been Holtfrerich who claims that there were other policies which would have improved the situation, but that Brüning chose not to apply them. He accepts that there were weaknesses in Weimar's economy, but he rejects the idea of a sick economy doomed to collapse even before the onset of the depression. In Holtfrerich's opinion, Brüning remained committed to his economic policy in spite of the alternative suggestions put forward by members of his own government. He took this line because existing policies were necessary to achieve his domestic and foreign policy aims. Brüning's real aim was to use the depression to prove to the Allies that the payment of reparations was no longer realistic. He also wanted to discredit and weaken the reputation of the Republic. It was not so much that circumstances prevented Brüning from facing the problems of the depression, it was simply that he had other aims in mind and his priorities lay elsewhere.

The debate about the conflicting interpretations put forward by Borchardt and Holtfrerich has been fierce and the outcome still has to be decided. Holtfrerich and his supporters have modified their interpretation by suggesting that Brüning did have other options that he might have followed, even if they were not as many as was once believed. Other economic measures in the summer of 1931, such as work creation schemes in the construction industry and the reduction of agricultural subsidies to make spending possible elsewhere, might just have been enough to lessen the worst effects of the depression during 1932. That these were rejected on political grounds because of Brüning's determination to show that Germany could not afford to pay reparations is also probably correct. However, Borchardt has succeeded in showing that there were no easy solutions to the crisis and that any alternative approach would have had serious consequences. Holtfrerich's alternatives are suggested with all the advantages of hindsight. Borchardt has rejected the criticism of Brüning made by many historians that the depression could have been better tackled by increased spending, especially at a time when it would have meant that Germany was acting differently from the rest of the world. He has also broadened the area of discussion beyond the narrow limits of 1929–32 and has shown the serious nature of the Weimar Republic's economic condition before the onset of the world depression. Borchardt's view is an attractive one and, despite some criticisms, he has changed the focus of debate on this period of history. His defence of Brüning's economic policy is convincing, although it is not yet universally accepted in all its details.

e) Brüning's removal from office

In the spring of 1932, Hindenburg's first seven-year term of office as President came to an end. Brüning committed himself to securing the old man's re-election and in spite of the campaign fought by the Nazis on behalf of their leader, Adolf Hitler, it was Hindenburg who won on the second ballot. He gained 19.3 million votes (53 per cent) compared with Hitler's 13.4 million (36.8 per cent). However, Hindenburg showed no gratitude to Brüning and, at the end of May 1932, the President forced his Chancellor to resign by refusing to sign any more emergency decrees. Why was this?

The immediate cause was the President's displeasure at Brüning's proposal to employ 600,000 unemployed workers on *Junker* estates in East Prussia. The landowners regarded the plan as 'agrarian bolshevism' and it resulted in Germany's social elite turning against Brüning. However, that was not the only cause of Brüning's downfall. By the end of 1931, confidence in Brüning had begun to wane as the effects of the depression began to take their toll. In June 1932, Germany was involved in a crisis when one of its major banks, the *Danat*, closed its doors to customers, meaning that all those who had their savings there were unable to gain access to them. By the end of the year unemployment was approaching five million and there were demonstrations in the streets. Doubts about Brüning were also beginning to emerge among those surrounding President Hindenburg. General Groener, the Defence Minister, later reflected:

1 I knew very well that the intention was to bring down the Chancellor.
In the course of the winter, the Reich President had twice mentioned
to me that Dr. Brüning did not quite represent his ideal as Reich
Chancellor. He did not accept my comment that at the moment he
5 would not find a better one. General von Schleicher had also made no
bones about the fact that he was thinking in terms of a change of
Chancellor. In view of his connections with the Reich President's
entourage, it can be assumed that he took part in the removal of Dr.
Brüning as Chancellor. During the absence of the Reich President in
10 Neudeck, his country estate, where Brüning's fall was decided upon,
General von Schleicher was in continual contact by telephone with
Hindenburg's son.

It is now generally agreed that the group surrounding the old man
had planned Brüning's fall from power. The scheming and ambitious
Kurt von Schleicher, recognising Brüning's limitations and unpopu-
larity, was convinced that the Nazis could no longer be ignored. He
wanted them to be included in a right-wing government that would
no longer have to depend on the Social Democrats. It is quite clear
from the diaries of the leading Nazi, Josef Goebbels, that during the
weeks before Brüning's resignation intrigue and rumour were already
rife:

1 8th May 1932
... The Führer (Adolf Hitler) has an important interview with Schleicher
in the presence of a few gentlemen of the President's immediate circle.
All goes well. The Führer has spoken decisively. Brüning's fall is
5 expected shortly. The President of the Reich will withdraw his confidence from him. The plan is to constitute a Presidential Cabinet. The
Reichstag will be dissolved. Repressive enactments are to be cancelled.
We shall be free to go ahead as we like, and mean to outdo ourselves
in propaganda.

10 11 May 1932
The Reichstag drags on. Groener's position is shaken; the army no
longer supports him. Even those with most to do with him urge his
downfall...

Brüning is trying to salvage what he can. He speaks in the Reichstag and
15 cleverly beats a retreat on foreign politics. There he becomes aggressive. He believes himself within sight of the goal. He does not mention
Groener at all. So he too has given him up! The whole debate turns on
the lifting of the ban on the SA. Groener strongly objects to this. It will
be his undoing.

20 24 May 1932
... Saturday will see the end of Brüning. Secretary of State Meissner
leaves for Neudeck. Now we must hope for the best. The list of
ministers is more or less settled: von Papen, Chancellor; von

Neurath, Foreign Minister, and then a list of unfamiliar names. The
25 main point as far as we are concerned is to ensure that the Reichstag
is dissolved...

30 May 1932
The bomb has exploded. Brüning has presented the resignation of his
entire Cabinet... The system has begun to crumble... Meet the Führer
30 at Nauen. The President wished to see him in the course of the after-
noon... The conference with the President went off well. The SA prohibition is going to be cancelled. Uniforms are to be allowed again. The
Reichstag is to be dissolved.

If one accepts that Brüning's fall was planned at an appropriate
moment by the intrigue of those around the President, one might be
tempted to view Brüning as an innocent sacrifice. However, it should
also be borne in mind that Brüning was in the end a victim of a situation that started before the winter of 1931–2 and which he himself
had lived with since 1930. Certainly, he was removed by the President
without reference to the *Reichstag*, but until that moment Brüning
had only survived as Chancellor because he enjoyed the backing of
Hindenburg. Brüning had agreed with the creation of presidential
government based on the powers granted by Article 48 of the constitution and this makes it hard to defend him when he later became the
victim of the intrigue of the presidential court.

f) Brüning: an assessment

Although Brüning was certainly no democrat, he was an honest, hard-
working and honourable man with a desire to help his country escape
from its crisis. His aims were firstly to end the payment of reparations
and to speed up the revision of the Treaty of Versailles and secondly
to reduce the powers of the *Reichstag* and eventually to set up an
authoritarian regime. In many respects Brüning was making good
progress towards these aims when he was dismissed. However, he was
not clever enough to appreciate how dangerous and unstable the
crisis had become in Germany by 1932. Neither did he realise how
insecure was his own position. Whilst Brüning retained the confidence of the President, presidential government protected his position. Unfortunately, he proved incapable of providing the nation
with the leadership it required in its hour of need. With no real hope
of improvement, it is not surprising that large sections of the population looked to the Nazis to save the situation. Brüning would have
nothing to do with Hitler and the Nazis and he continued to uphold
the rule of law. Sadly, presidential rule had allowed the old elites to
influence government and, at the same time, made the German
people used to rule by decree. In this way democracy was undermined
and the way was cleared for more extreme political parties to assume
power. In the end, it is hard to escape the conclusion that Brüning's

chancellorship was a dismal failure. In view of the Nazi tyranny that was soon to come, Brüning's failure was a tragic one.

3 The Rise of National Socialism

> **KEY ISSUE** For what reasons did so many Germans vote for the Nazi Party?

The rise of National Socialism is an important feature of the years 1929–33 and it must be considered as an important factor in the events leading to the collapse of the Weimar Republic. Although in the early 1920s it had only been a fringe party, during the period 1929–33, the Nazi Party emerged as a mass movement. In the *Reichstag* election of July 1932, it polled 37.4 per cent of the vote. Although Hitler did not come to power as a result of an election, it is true that his party's electoral strength gave it a power base that, in the last years of the Weimar Republic's existence, could not be ignored.

a) Nazi ideology

The political and racial theories of the Nazis were not original. In many ways, its ideology differed little from a host of other right-wing groups in Germany in the early 1920s. It was a mixture of strong nationalism, imperialism as expressed in *Lebensraum*, and racism. It was violently anti-Semitic and considered the German people to be part of a superior Aryan master race. Such ideas were to be found in the cheap, crudely written pamphlets sold to the masses in the streets of the large cities as well as to students in German universities. Their theories also formed the basis of the views held by influential pressure groups, such as the Pan-German League. As a set of political ideas, Nazism lacked any real intellectual depth. It was not even well thought out since it contained glaring contradictions. However, in spite of this, the Nazis succeeded, more than any other group, in becoming the most outspoken opponents of the Weimar Republic. The Nazi scapegoats were the Jews, the communists, the socialists and

Nazi representation in the *Reichstag*	
1924 (1)	32
1924 (2)	14
1928	12
1930	107
1932 (1)	230
1932 (2)	196
1933	288

the liberals. All were identified with Weimar democracy and blamed as being responsible for Germany's condition.

b) The organisation and appeal of the Nazi Party

By 1929, at the start of final crisis that faced the Republic, the Nazi Party was in a much stronger position to take advantage of its position as the 'we told you so' party. After the failure of the Munich *Putsch* of 1923, Hitler used his time in prison to write *Mein Kampf* (My Struggle). On his release he worked to rebuild and restructure the party with the intention of coming to power by legal means. Most important was his reorganisation of the Party according to *führerprinzip*, the principle of *führer* power. This reduced differences within the Party, strengthened Hitler's own position and reorganised the structure of the Party throughout Germany. By this system, the responsibility for the Party in a particular region was placed in the hands of a *Gauleiter*, a regional party boss, who was responsible to Hitler alone. At the same time the Nazis recognised the importance of what has been called 'associationism'. The Party tried to extend its influence in various organisations and so counteract the influence of the opposed views of socialism and Catholicism. 'Associated' organisations were created for teachers, students, doctors, craftsmen and a host of other groups. The Party also developed a clear identity by the use of flags, uniforms, salutes and insignia. Impressive meetings and rallies were arranged and attempts were made to indoctrinate the people into accepting the Nazi view. All these activities were supported by impressive speeches and the use of propaganda. As a result, by 1929 party membership stood at nearly 100,000 and most of the other right-wing racist groups in Germany had been swallowed up. The Nazis had created a party machine capable of winning the support of large sections of the German people.

Research into who actually voted for the Nazis and the reasons for this has become a major historical study. The view that National Socialism was a middle-class movement, although still containing a fair amount of truth, is now considered too simple an explanation. Instead, it is now generally believed that the key feature of Nazi electoral support was the Party's ability to appeal to all sections of German society. Unlike many other parties in Germany, the Nazis were not limited by regional, denominational and class ties, and were thus able to establish a broad cross-section of support. By 1932, they were the only party which could claim to have widespread support in every region of the country. In short, the NSDAP became Germany's first genuine *Volkspartei*, or people's party. However, the extent of Nazi support should not hide the fact that certain groups were more attracted to Nazism than others. In mainly Roman Catholic areas, the popularity of the Nazis was less marked than in Protestant regions. Likewise, the Nazis had greater support in the countryside and in the residential suburbs than in the large industrial cities. These trends were probably the result of the Nazis finding it much harder to break down the traditional loyalties of working-class and Catholic communities. They found it easier to win support in Protestant and rural areas where middle-class loyalties were less strong and people were perhaps more likely to accept the Nazi message.

Despite these regional variations, National Socialism developed into a genuinely national mass movement, appealing to different social groups. This tends to support the view that it used different methods to appeal to different sections of the community. To some, Nazism could appear new and exciting; to others, it was traditional and reassuring. It claimed to be against both capitalism and socialism. Above all, it was both revolutionary and reactionary, since it wished to destroy the Republic and at the same time promised a return to a glorious bygone age; it could be regarded as both revolutionary and reactionary. The fact that it appeared to be all things to all men was at the heart of Nazi electoral success. National Socialism was further strengthened by the spectacular success of Josef Goebbels' propaganda machine, which encouraged the acceptance of two ideas. The first was the Führer cult in which Hitler was portrayed as a messiah-type figure sent to save Germany; the second was the idea of *Volksgemeinschaft,* a People's Community, which promised to create a truly national community bridging all class and social divisions. Consequently, when the world economic crisis struck the already weak and unstable Weimar Republic, National Socialism was ideally placed to benefit. As it flourished, so the Republic's chances of survival diminished.

4 The Final Months of the Weimar Republic

> **KEY ISSUE** What part did political intrigue play during the final months prior to the appointment of Hitler as Chancellor?

From Brüning's fall in May 1932 until Hitler's appointment as Chancellor in January 1933 Germany's destiny was decided by the intrigue of a few key personalities surrounding President Hindenburg. This had been the case under Brüning, but under chancellors Franz von Papen (May–December 1932) and Kurt von Schleicher (December 1932–January 1933), it became even more marked. What were the aims of this conservative nationalist clique? Why did they fail to produce a political solution that could have prevented Hitler's coming to power?

Brüning had recognised that government by decree was not the answer to Germany's problems. He had considered the possibility of restoring the Hohenzollern monarchy in the form of Wilhelm II's son as a means of winning popularity and resisting the appeal of Nazism.

His idea received little support. For a while, von Papen headed a cabinet dominated by aristocratic landowners and industrialists, which soon earned the nickname of the 'cabinet of barons'. In September, his cabinet suffered a massive vote of no confidence by 512 votes to 42. In his frustration he proposed a 'fighting programme' by the end of 1932, in which he intended to use the army and police to get rid of parliament once and for all, to crush all political parties and to force through a new authoritarian constitution. Bearing in mind the violence between the rival paramilitary organisations at this time, the introduction of such a plan would have risked a civil war. Papen found himself without any real support even from within the presidential circle.

The aim of Weimar's last chancellor, Kurt von Schleicher, was what has been termed 'a policy of the diagonal'. This was his plan to create a more broadly based government that, by attracting the support of the socialist wing of the NSDAP, would split the Nazis. In this way, Schleicher hoped to show himself to be a chancellor of national reconciliation. His plans came to nothing. In this situation, Hindenburg finally agreed, on the suggestion of Papen, to appoint Adolf Hitler as Chancellor in the mistaken belief that Hitler could be controlled and used in the interests of the conservative establishment.

The various attempts to solve Germany's crisis in 1932–3 all came to nothing because of a lack of popular support. Germany was a modern society and it was no longer so easy to brush aside the wishes of the people. Nazi political strength was only too apparent in the election results, and their exclusion from government at a time of great distress simply led to violence in the streets between the various paramilitary groups. This in turn increased the atmosphere of crisis. By January 1933 the men around President Hindenburg were divided and no longer capable of governing the country. In the end, they simply ran out of alternatives and were no longer able to exclude Hitler and the Nazis.

5 Why Did Weimar Democracy Fail?

> **KEY ISSUE** Which factors contributed to the collapse of the Weimar Republic?

a) The collapse of the Weimar Republic – an overall view

It is now clear that when Hitler became Chancellor on 30 January 1933, Weimar democracy was already dead. The problem for the historian is trying to determine when the Weimar Republic actually expired and why. In the view of some, Weimar had been a gamble with no chance of success. For others, the Republic continued to offer the chance of democratic survival until mid-1932 when von

Papen became Chancellor. In the July elections, the Nazis became the largest party in the *Reichstag* and although they were without an overall majority this marked the end of the Republic. Views of the reasons for Weimar's collapse differ and over the years historians have emphasised different aspects or applied different criteria.

From the start, the Weimar Republic was faced by the hostility of Germany's established elites. Following military defeat and the threat of revolution, this opposition was at first limited. However, the fact that so many figures in German society and business rejected the idea of a democratic republic and worked against the interests of Weimar in the hope that there would be a return to pre-1914 situation was a major weakness. This was a powerful handicap to the successful development of the Republic in the 1920s and in the 1930s and it was to become a decisive factor in its final collapse. The Republic was also troubled by almost continuous economic crisis that affected all levels of society. It inherited the enormous costs and effects of the First World War as well as the burden of post-war reconstruction, Allied reparations and the huge cost of pensions. So, even though the inflation crisis of 1923–4 was overcome, problems in the economy remained unresolved. These were to have dramatic consequences with the onset of the world economic crisis in 1929.

Weimar democracy never enjoyed widespread political support. There was never total acceptance of and confidence in its system and its values. From the Republic's birth its narrow base of popular support was caught between the extremes of left and right. As time went by, Weimar's claims to be the legitimate government became increasingly open to question. Sadly, Weimar democracy was associated with defeat and the humiliation of the Treaty of Versailles and reparations. Its reputation was further damaged by the crisis of 1922–3. It is significant that, by 1928, German liberalism, which should have provided additional support for the Republic, was in decline. At the same time, the Centre and DNVP were both moving to the right. Even the loyalty and the commitment of the SPD, Weimar's largest party up to 1932, to democracy has to be balanced against the fact after 1924, it was never a coalition partner and was at loggerheads with its left-wing partner, the KPD. In short, a sizeable proportion of the German population had lost faith in the existing constitutional arrangements and was looking for change. In this chapter, we have examined the events that finally brought the years of the Weimar Republic to an end. It is now time to look back over the years 1919–33, which proved to be such a difficult period in German history. During this time Weimar democracy went through a number of phases. The difficult circumstances of its birth in 1918–19 left it handicapped and it was in many respects a major achievement that it survived the problems of the period 1919–23. However, the years of relative stability from 1923 to 1929 amounted to only a short breathing space and did not result in any strengthening of the Weimar system. On the eve of the world economic crisis it seems that Weimar's long-term chances of survival were already far from good. In the end, the impact of the world depression increased the pressures that brought about Weimar's final crisis. The manner of Brüning's appointment and his decision to rule by emergency decree created another system of government, a regime backed by presidential decree. This was followed in 1932 by the electoral breakthrough of the Nazis. From this time democracy's chance of surviving was slim indeed. Briefly, the flame of democracy continued to burn but with ever decreasing brightness. In January 1933, the Nazis finally extinguished it but, in truth, democratic rule in Germany had died some time before, in the spring and summer of 1930.

Summary Diagram
Weimar: the Final Years

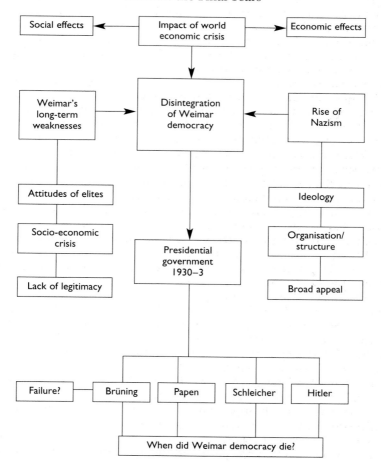

Working on Chapter 9

In this chapter you have studied a period of German history that had the most dire consequences. It ended with the country edging towards a dictatorship that was a prelude to the coming of tyranny and genocide. There are several important issues for you to think about. The main one on which you need to concentrate is the reasons for the collapse the Weimar Republic. It is also important that you give thought to the opportunities that were created which allowed Hitler and the Nazis to come to power. There are many reasons to be considered – the legacy of defeat, the humiliation of the Treaty of Versailles, the frailty of German democracy, political instability and a series of economic disasters. Be sure that you can account for the weakness of the German party system. Why did the parties fail to unite to form an effective government? Why did the parties of the centre and right fail to form workable coalitions? Remember the Nazis came to power without ever winning an overall majority at the polls! The historian Alan Bullock wrote, 'Hitler did not seize power; he was jobbed into office by backstairs intrigue'. Do you agree? Finally, it would be useful to draw up a profile of the main political parties contesting the elections on 1932 and analyse the reasons why different groups of Germans voted for them. In doing this pay particular attention to the reasons why so many supported the Nazis.

Structured questions on Chapter 9

1. **a)** Why did the Wall Street Crash come to have such a catastrophic impact on the German economy? (*5 marks*)
   b) In what ways did the recession affect the lives of working-class Germans? (*5 marks*)
   c) For what reasons did President Hindenburg use Article 48 of the constitution in 1930? (*5 marks*)
   d) Why was Brüning removed from office in 1932? (*5 marks*)

2. **a)** What is meant by i) *Lebensraum* and ii) *Volksgemeinschaft*? (*2×2 = 4 marks*)
   b) How did the Nazis use 'associationism' to win support? (*5 marks*)
   c) What did von Schleicher hope to achieve when he was appointed chancellor in 1932? (*6 marks*)
   d) Why did popular support for Hitler and the Nazis increase during this period? (*10 marks*)

Essay questions on Chapter 9

1. 'At best, weak and, at worse, grossly incompetent'. How valid is this assessment of Brüning?

2. Was the rise of the Nazi Party the main reason for the final collapse of the Weimar Republic? Explain your answer fully.

Answering synoptic questions

The word synoptic means to take an overall view. A synoptic-type question will require you to illustrate your knowledge and understanding of an extended period of history, in this case over the years 1890–1933. Such questions will most likely follow an ongoing theme. You will need to use a range of historical concepts and show your ability to analyse and develop an argument. Some topics covered by this book that might be used as the basis for synoptic questioning include:

economic developments;
the struggle to achieve democratic government;
foreign policy;
the role of opposition and dissent.

Let us consider the possible content of answers to synoptic questions based on two of these topics.

How successful were attempts to introduce democratic government in Germany during the period 1890–1933?	**Did German foreign policy succeed in achieving its aims during the period 1890–1933?**
The legacy of Bismarck's constitution.	Bismarck's foreign policy and his system of alliances.
Wilhelm II and his court. The move towards the Kaiser's personal rule.	German world policy – *Weltpolitik*.
The influence of the elites in maintaining the status quo.	The disclosures of the *Daily Telegraph* Affair.
The decline of the Kaiser's influence during the First World War. Germany as a military dictatorship.	German militarism.
	Germany's search for allies – Austria-Hungary and Turkey.

How successful were attempts to introduce democratic government in Germany during the period 1890–1933?	Did German foreign policy succeed in achieving its aims during the period 1890–1933?
The rise of the (socialist) SPD.	
Post-war chaos. The left and the German revolution of 1918-19.	Anglo-German relations. Colonial and naval rivalry.
The birth of the Weimar Republic and the new republic's constitution.	Policy at the time of the Moroccan crises of 1905 and 1911.
The threat from the extreme left and right. The Ebert–Groener pact.	Reaction to events in 1914. The 'blank cheque'.
The Kapp and Munich *putsches*.	The Schlieffen Plan and the repercussions of its failure.
The instability of coalition governments.	The policy of *Siegfriede*.
The problems that beset the Weimar Republic. Party differences.	Post-war problems and the reaction to Versailles.
Hopes of Müller's 'Grand Coalition', 1929.	The policy of 'fulfilment'. The Treaty of Rapallo, 1922.
The failure of Brüning and the introduction of government by presidential decree.	Stresemann – his foreign policy aims.
Years of political intrigue and the impact of the rise of Hitler and the Nazi Party.	The Dawes Plan (1924), Locarno (1925) and Kellogg–Briand (1928).
The end of Weimar democracy.	Membership of the League of Nations.
	The appeal of Nazi foreign policy pledges.

Glossary

ADV	Alldeutsche Verband. Pan-German League. Right-wing nationalist interest group.
Anschluss	Union. Unification of Germany and Austria.
Beamte	State official.
BdL	Bund der Landwirte. Farmers' League. Lobby for high tariffs.
Burgfriede	Political truce.
Diktat	Right-wing description of Versailles Treaty. Literally, a 'dictated' peace.
Ersatzkaiser	Literally 'substitute kaiser'. A reference given to the powers endowed upon the Weimar presidency.
Flottenverein	Navy League. Nationalist interest group set up to press for increased naval spending.
Führerprinzip	The leadership principle.
Gau	Region. Basic unit of Nazi organization.
Junker	Prussian landowner.
Kaiserreich	Imperial Germany 1871–1918.
KRA	Kriegsrohstoffabteilung. War raw materials department.
Kulturkampf	Cultural struggle. Bismarck's anti-Catholic policy of the 1870s.
Landtag	Provincial parliament.
Lebensraum	Living-space. Policy of expansion into eastern Europe.
Mittelstand	Middle class. Traditionally reference to the artisan/shopkeeper rather than the new industrialists.
OHL	Oberste Heeresleitung. Supreme Army Command.
Rechtsstaat	Constitutional state based upon the rule of law.
Reichsrat	Second chamber of German parliament, representing federal provinces.
Rentenmark	New currency introduced in 1924.
Sammlungspolitik	Literally a 'policy of concentration'. Term used by structuralists to describe the attempt by the elites to rally the middle and upper classes behind the imperial regime.
Sonderweg	Special path. Used in various senses to suggest that German history was different to the norm.
Spartakusbund	Group of extreme left-wing socialists.
Spartakist League	Forerunner of Communist Party.
Weltpolitik	Literally 'world policy'. Initiative launched by German government in 1897.

Further Reading

1 Textbooks

Because of the importance of Germany in modern European history there are a number of suitable general textbooks in print. By far the most thorough and readable surveys are: **William Carr**, *A History of Germany 1815–1990* (Edward Arnold, 4th ed. 1992). **David Evans and Jane Jenkins**, *Years of Weimar and the Third Reich* (Hodder & Stoughton, 1999) Chapters 1–5. More intellectually demanding are **Volker Berghahn**, *Modern Germany* (CUP, 2nd ed. 1987), and **Gordon Craig**, *Germany 1866–1945* (OUP, 1981).

The emphasis and approach of these four books varies quite considerably. It would be a good idea to see if you can detect these differences by dipping into one or two of the relevant chapters of each book. You should not take detailed notes from them, but you could briefly note the 'line' taken by each author on the major issues.

2 Biographies

Because of the influence of the 'structuralist' school and its dislike of 'personalising' history, German academic historians have tended to fight shy of the biographical approach. As a result, no full-scale biography of Wilhelm II has ever been written by a German university historian. The same can also be said of Brüning and Hindenburg. Stresemann and Ebert have not been so completely ignored, but none of the works have been translated. However, if you would like to gain a feel for some of the personalities refer to: **J.C.G. Röhl**, *The Kaiser and his Court* (Cambridge, 1994). This is a stimulating and scholarly work based on an exhaustive analysis of original sources. Particularly recommended are Chapters 1, 4 and 7. **J. Wright**, 'Stresemann and Weimar' in *History Today*, October, 1989. A brief, but excellent article which reassesses his career.

3 Specialist Studies

If you wish to study some of the historical controversies more deeply you will need to select your reading with great care. The academic literature on German history is immense and much of it is detailed and very specialised. The following are suggested 'starting-points':
H-U. Wehler, *The German Empire* (Leamington Spa, 1984). This is a difficult read, even in translation. The most useful parts for you to read would probably be pp. 52–99 and 192–246.
V. Berghahn, *Germany and the Approach of War in 1914* (London, 1973).
R. Evans, 'Kaiser Wilhelm and German History' in *History Review* Issues 10 and 11 in 1991. A good review of the main themes.

F. Fischer, *From Kaiserreich to Third Reich* (Unwin & Hyman, 1986). The best brief introduction to Fischer's thinking. It is only 99 pages long.
E. Kolb, *The Weimar Republic* (Unwin & Hyman, 1988). A thorough and clearly written historical and historiographical survey.
D. Peukert, *The Weimar Republic* (Penguin, 1991). An original and thought-provoking approach.
A. de Jonge, *The Weimar Chronicle.* Not really a history book, but an attempt to capture the mood of Weimar Germany.
I. Kershaw (ed), *Weimar; Why did German Democracy Fail?* (Weidenfeld & Nicholson, 1990). Mainly concentrates on the economic aspects of the debate.
A.J. Nicholls, *Weimar and the Rise of Hitler* (Macmillan, 3rd ed. 1991).

4 Sources

There is no definitive collection of documents in English covering the whole period 1890–1933, but a good range of material is provided by:
J. Laver (ed.), *Imperial and Weimar Germany 1890–1933* (Hodder & Stoughton, 1992).
J.C.G. Röhl, *From Bismarck to Hitler* (Longmans, 1970). For a full range of statistical data turn to:
V.Berghahn, see above, pp. 269–312. 55 tables on politics, economics and social trends.

Index

Agrarian League 33, 36
agriculture 14, 15, 68, 78, 125, 126
Alsace-Lorraine 4, 102, 126
Angell, W.A., *The Recovery of Germany*
    124–5
army 41–2, 56, 73–4, 91, 93, 113,
    114–15, 115–18, 120, 121, 135
Austria, and the German
    Confederation 1–2
Austria–Hungary 47, 48, 51, 53, 54,
    55–6, 57, 64

balance of payments, Imperial
    Germany 11, 12
Balkan Wars (1912–13) 51, 53
Bavaria, socialist republic
    proclaimed in 85, 87, 91, 113
Berghahn, Volker 78, 107
Bethmann-Hollweg, Theobald von
    20, 21–2, 40–1, 42, 51, 52, 53,
    54, 55, 57, 65, 69, 72–3, 79–80
Bismarck, Otto von 1–6, 16, 18, 22,
    23, 25, 32, 46, 47–8
Boer War 48, 50
Borchardt, Karl 127–8, 152, 153
Bosnian Crisis (1908–9) 21, 51
Brest–Litovsk, Treaty of (1918) 69,
    70, 80–2, 102, 120
Britain 48–9, 50, 51–2, 56, 64–5, 68,
    69, 70, 101, 102
Brüning, Heinrich 130, 149–56,
    158–9, 161
budget problems 36, 37, 126
Bullock, Alan 162
Bülow, Bernhard von 7, 17, 19,
    20–1, 34, 36–7, 38–9, 40, 42, 44,
    51
Bundesrat (Federal Council) 4

Caprivi, Count Leo von 20, 32–4, 36,
    43, 44
cartels, and the German economy
    12–13, 125
Centre Party 13, 23–5, 26, 33, 36–7,
    80, 128, 129, 130, 160
Churchill, Winston 17

class 13–15, 25, 79, 108–10, 148,
    157, 158
Clemenceau, Georges 102
coal industry 9, 10, 125
Constitution 4–6, 18, 23–5, 97–100,
    120, 121, 146, 149–50, 155
constitutional reforms (1918) 86–7
Craig, Gordon 99

Daily Telegraph affair 37–40, 43, 44,
    72, 87
Dawes Plan (1924) 118, 119, 121,
    123, 126, 137–8
DNVP (German National People's
    Party) 96, 114, 121, 128, 129,
    130–1, 160
Drexler, Anton 114

Ebert, Friedrich 85, 88, 90, 91–2, 93,
    116
economy *see* German economy
education 12
Ehrhardt, Hermann 115
Ellensburg, Prinz Philipp zu 17
Elliott, B.J. 17
Erfurt Congress (1891) 25
Erzberger, Matthias 80, 115, 130, 135
Eulenburg, Count Philip 19, 34, 37,
    43

Falkenhayn, Erich von 55, 64, 65, 73
Fatherland Party 80
First World War   16–17, 46–7,
    53–6, 56–8, 61–84, 85, 92,
    106–7, 135
Fischer, Fritz 26, 47, 49–50, 52, 58
food supplies, and the First World
    War 66, 68, 78
France 48, 50, 52, 52–3, 56, 58, 62,
    65, 101, 102, 107–8, 118, 136–7,
    138–9
Frank, Bruno 71
Franz Ferdinand, Archduke,
    assassination of 53–4
Frederick III, Emperor of Germany
    2

Freikorps 91, 93, 113, 114–15, 121

German Confederation 1–2
German economy 5–6, 9–12, 66–8,
    82, 83, 105–12, 119, 120, 121,
    124–8, 134, 137–8, 141–2,
    147–8, 151–3, 160, 161
German nationalism 35, 49, 79
German Revolution (1918–19) 83,
    85–94
Goebbels, Josef 154–5, 158
Groener, General Wilhelm 91, 93,
    153–4

Haldane, Lord 53
health, effects of Weimar Republic
    inflation on 111
Heuss, Theodor 100
Hindenburg, Oskar von 151
Hindenburg, Paul von 17, 65, 69, 70,
    73, 74, 75, 123, 131, 146, 149,
    153–5, 159
Hitler, Adolf 74, 75, 76–7, 98, 99,
    100, 114, 118, 121, 154, 157,
    158, 159
Hohenlohe-Schillingfurst, Prince
    Choldwig 20, 34, 36
Holstein, Friedrich von 34
Holtfrerich, C.L. 110, 111, 127, 152
Holy Roman Empire 1
Hugenberg, Alfred 131

Imperial Germany 5–6, 9–12, 12–13,
    15–23, 28–9, 35 *see also* Wilhelm
    II, Emperor of Germany (the
    Kaiser)
industrial disputes 76, 142
industrial production 9–11, 125
inflation, and the Weimar Republic
    105–12

Junkers (nobility) 14, 15, 27, 29, 153

Kaas, Ludwig 130
Kapp, Wolfgang 115
Kapp–Lüttwitz *Putsch* (1920) 115–18,
    120, 121, 135

Kellogg–Briand Pact 123, 139
Kennedy, P. 43
Kolb, E. 140–1
KPD (German Communist Party) 88,
    91, 97, 112–13, 128, 129, 160
Kruger Telegram 48, 49
Kulturkampf 2

labour force, in Imperial Germany
    11
League of Nations 101, 139
Lebensraum 49, 156
Liebknecht, Karl 89, 91
Lloyd George, David 58
Locarno, Treaty of (1925) 138–9
Ludendorff, Erich 17, 65, 69, 70, 73,
    74, 75, 85–6, 118
Luther, Hans 129
Luxemburg, Rosa 89, 91

Marx, Wilhelm 129
Max, Prince of Baden 85, 86, 87, 90
Meissner, Otto 151
Michaelis, Georg 73, 80
Miquel, Johannes von 34
Moltke, Helmuth von 55, 56, 64, 75
Moroccan Crisis (1905–6) 21, 50
Moroccan Crisis (1911) 41, 47, 51,
    52
Müller, Hermann 128, 129, 130, 149

National Liberals 14
navy, German 36, 50, 51–2, 87
Nazis (National Socialists) 98, 114,
    128, 131, 146, 150, 152, 155–6,
    156–8, 159, 160, 161
Nicholls, A.J. 131
November Revolution *see* German
    Revolution (1918–19)

`Organisation Council' gang 115

Pan-German League 35, 49, 79, 156
Papen, Franz von 158, 159–60
Poincaré, Raymond 107
political parties 23, 24, 25–6, 95–7,
    112–14, 128–32, 142

population 10, 11–12, 126
Posadowsky-Wehner, Count 34
Preuss, Hugo 104–5
proportional representation 98
Prussia 1–2, 4–5

Rapallo, Treaty of (1922) 134, 137
Rathenau, Walter 66, 115, 135
Reichstag 5–6, 23–5, 26, 28, 33, 41,
    74, 80, 82, 86–7, 98, 99, 128,
    150, 156
Reinsurance Treaty 48
Remarque, Erich Maria 109
Riezler, K. 54
Ritter, Gerhard 58
Röhl, John 19, 57
Roman Catholic Church 2, 13, 37,
    157, 158
Ruhr occupation (1923) 108, 118,
    138
Russia 48, 49, 54, 55–6, 58, 62–3,
    64, 69, 80, 102, 134, 137, 139

Sammlungspolitik 27, 28
Scheidemann, Philipp 88
Schleicher, Kurt von 151, 154, 158,
    159
Schlieffen, Alfred von 56, 62, 75
Seeckt, General Hans von 116, 117,
    132–3
Shirer, William 123–4
social welfare 125
Spartacist League (later KPD) 85,
    88, 89–90, 91, 95, 115
SPD (Social Democratic Party) 2,
    24, 25–6, 33, 34, 36–7, 41, 56,
    71, 73, 79, 80, 86, 88, 91, 92, 97,
    112, 128, 129–30, 131, 150
steel industry 9, 10, 125
Stinnes, Hugo 109
Stinnes–Legien agreement 91
Stresemann, Gustav 108, 118–20,
    121, 130, 134–40
structuralist historians 26–7, 49, 56
Stülpnagel, Colonel 132

tariff reform 33, 36, 37
taxation 41, 68
Tirpitz, Admiral von 34, 35–6, 51,
    65, 80
Triple Entente 21

unemployment 15, 110, 125, 126,
    147, 148, 153
unification of Germany 1–2
United States 69, 70, 80, 83, 128,
    146, 147, 148
USPD (Independent Social
    Democratic Party) 80, 82, 88,
    90, 91, 92, 97, 112, 128

Versailles, Treaty of (1919) 46–7,
    58, 85, 100–5, 114,
120, 121, 126, 132–4, 155, 160

wages 15, 76, 109–10, 125
'War Council' meeting (1912) 53
Wehler, H.U. 26–7, 86
Weimar Republic 28, 48, 61, 87,
    91–2, 95–164, *see also* Versailles,
    Treaty of (1919)
Weltpolitik (imperialism) 27, 34–7,
    40, 44, 46, 47, 49–51, 57, 58,
    135

Wilhelm I, Emperor of Germany 2,
    22
Wilhelm II, Emperor of Germany
    (the Kaiser) 2, 3, 4, 15–23,
    26–7, 29, 32, 33–4, 35, 37–9,
    40, 42–3, 46, 48, 63, 72–3, 85,
    86, 87, 90
Wilson, Woodrow, and the Fourteen
    Points 101, 102
Wirth, Josef 130, 133–4
world trade, and the Weimar
    Republic 125–6

Young Plan 123, 131, 139, 140, 146

Zabern affair (1913) 41–2, 56, 87